D1174432

# Cult of the Sun

# Rosalie David

# *Cult of the Sun*

## Myth and Magic in Ancient Egypt

**J. M. Dent & Sons Ltd**
London Melbourne Toronto

First published 1980
© Rosalie David 1980

Printed in Great Britain by
Biddles Ltd, Guildford, Surrey for
J M Dent & Sons Ltd
Aldine House, 33 Welbeck Street, London
Phototypeset in 11/13 pt V.I.P. Bembo by
Western Printing Services Ltd, Bristol

British Library Cataloguing in Publication Data

David, Rosalie
    Cult of the sun
    1 Ra (Egyptian deity)
    2 Sun (in religion, folk-lore, etc) – Egypt
    I Title
    299'.31    BL2450.R2

ISBN 0-460-04284-X

# Contents

# List of Plates

# List of Line Drawings

# Acknowledgments

The sun cult in Egypt reached its zenith during the great period of pyramid construction and an attempt to draw together the threads of this worship must owe a considerable debt to previous research relating to this topic. Dr I. E. S. Edward's classic *The Pyramids of Egypt* has been an invaluable source of information and illustrative material in this respect.

I should like to express my thanks to Mr E. Bellis whose line drawings elucidate many points in the text; some of these drawings are adapted from other publications and due acknowledgment is made in each case in the List of Line Drawings. I am also most grateful to Mr W. Thomas of the Manchester Museum and Mr P. A. Clayton for enabling me to include the photographs of sites and objects in this book.

Finally, I should like to thank the publishers for their support and cooperation throughout the production of this book.

A. R. David

# 1 The Land of the Sun

In antiquity, two great natural forces influenced the destiny of one of the greatest civilizations the world has seen: the sun and the River Nile may be regarded as the two factors which affected the most basic concepts and beliefs of the ancient Egyptians.

Today, the traveller who visits Egypt for the first time and by air will be overwhelmingly impressed by the vivid contrast between the green, fertile Nile Valley and Delta region (which forms the mouth of the Nile where it flows into the Mediterranean Sea) and the barren desert which engulfs the cultivation and stretches away as far as the eye can see. The annual rainfall is almost non-existent in Upper Egypt and in the Delta region insufficient to support people, their animals and crops. The land is only made habitable by the phenomenon of the annual inundation. The situation is aptly described by an ancient Classical writer who called Egypt 'the gift of the Nile'.

The spring rains of tropical Africa and the melting snows on the Abyssinian uplands together swell the waters of the Blue Nile. Until recent times and the development of modern technology, the floods followed their course along the length of the river, the rushing waters first making their power felt at Aswan in southern Egypt at the end of June and finally reaching Cairo in northern Egypt in September. The flood then gradually subsided and the waters reached their lowest level in the following April. A successful harvest and the subsequent rejoicing or bewailing of the Egyptians was dependent upon the volume of water; a low Nile could mean famine but heavy floods would also bring disaster and destruction in their wake. In ancient times, the Nile was regarded as a god capable of providing Egypt with good and plentiful harvests but who was also a capricious benefactor to be worshipped and placated. Modern developments have removed the total dependency on the whims of nature, for modern dams, including the famous High Dam at Aswan, have been constructed along the river, and these regulate the flow of water required to irrigate the land through a series of canals. Nevertheless to grow crops on this fertile land, the farmer must also patiently and diligently irrigate and prepare the soil.

The basic methods of irrigation which are still in use were first devised in Egypt perhaps as early as the Predynastic period (before 3100 BC) and certainly at the beginning of the Historic period (c.3100 BC). The river banks were built up to prevent flooding and loss of precious water while canals were cut to divert the water into barren areas and provide more land for grazing and crops. The success of the system depended upon the constant maintenance of the dikes, and also, to be effective, it was necessary to carry out irrigation along the entire length of the Nile. The common agricultural needs of the communities living along the Nile Valley were so important that eventually the irrigation programme created a bond between people of different religious beliefs and politics and made Egypt into the first State.

The pulsating energy of the great river is an inescapable presence in Egypt, but even more dominant, regulating periods of work and rest and sinking below the horizon in unparalleled magnificence every night, the sun was a constant and omnipotent force to the ancient Egyptians. The Nile, although it played a vital role in the religious beliefs, politics, and economic and social development of the country, never achieved greatness as a deity. Hapy, the Nile-god, and other deities associated with the Nile did not rise to eminence amongst the gods of the Egyptian pantheon. The life-giving properties of the river were somewhat eclipsed by the bounties of Osiris, who was primarily a vegetation god who came to symbolize re-birth in both the annual re-growth of the vegetation after the subsidence of the floods and in the resurrection of individual souls after death. The sun, however, although regarded as distant and mysterious, became one of Egypt's greatest deities, regarded as the supreme creator and sustainer of life. It was the sun-cult which, at the end of the Eighteenth dynasty, flowered into a form of monotheism.

The belief that life continued after death and that man required preparation for his fate seems to have been part of the Egyptian consciousness from earliest times, possibly because of the unique combination of geographic and climatic conditions found in Egypt. The periodic processes of life and death could be observed in both the cycles of the sun and the land. The nightly death of the sun and its reappearance at dawn and the annual destruction and re-birth of the vegetation after the inundation may have prompted the Egyptians to consider that the human state reflected these processes of nature. Man's new existence after re-birth was nevertheless closely linked with this world, although the form it was believed to take varied throughout Egypt's long history. This basis to religious practice in Egypt may have been inspired by certain early discoveries which were a direct result of the environmental conditions and the powerful effect of the sun.

The ancient Egyptians called their country *Kemet* which meant the 'Black Land', referring to the colour of the soil which had been fertilized by the Nile mud and which supported the people, their animals and nurtured the crops. Beyond this there lay the desert areas, which were called *Deshret*, meaning the 'Red Land', similarly relating to the colour of the sand and rocks of this inhospitable region. Cultivated land was so precious to the Egyptians that, from earliest times the bodies of the dead were not buried within the community but were removed to the desert and placed in shallow graves in the sand. The fertile, cultivated soil could thus be reserved and fully utilized for the needs of the living. The dual effect of the sun's heat and the dryness of the sand brought about natural desiccation of the dead bodies. This process, apparently achieved unintentionally, eliminated the body fluids. The skin and often the hair remained on the bodies, preserving an almost lifelike appearance. Such a discovery probably happened when the bodies were accidentally uncovered some time after interment, perhaps as the result of the activities of scavenging jackals who were a constant menace to the cemeteries, or the drifting of the wind-blown sand. Instead of the expected skeletal form these desiccated corpses retained something of the original appearance of the deceased. This phenomenon must have profoundly affected the Egyptians' concept of life after death, and they carried to an unequalled degree the belief that a man needed his body, preserved in a recognizable state, in the next life. Every effort was made to safeguard and preserve the body to serve its owner throughout eternity.

The preparations for the afterlife became increasingly elaborate;

bodies were placed in brick-lined tombs, and this led to the decomposition of the skin and soft tissues, for the body was now no longer in direct contact with the desiccating and absorbent sand. Decomposition of the tissues occurred before the body had become desiccated. However, by this period, religious thinking demanded that the body should be preserved for use by its owner after death and the Egyptians eventually developed a more sophisticated method of preserving the body – a process we know today as 'mummification'.

By the beginning of the Historic period (c.3100 BC), a people had emerged who were profoundly aware of the correspondence between life and death. Survival and decay surrounded them, starkly illustrated by their immediate environment, where it was possible to take a step from the life-giving soil of the cultivated region into the arid desert and all its associations with death. However, observation of the natural cycles of the sun and the land also impressed upon the Egyptian mind the idea that life, death and re-birth were but stages in a process which followed an inevitable course. Vegetation deities and fertility rites united with the solar cult to form the foundation of their religion, and although the development of these elements was to some extent distinct, they nevertheless met and fused together in the concept that individual human life continued after death.

# 2  The rise of the Sun-God

A glance at a map of Egypt will confirm that, compared with other ancient civilizations in the ancient Near East, Egypt occupied a position which was geographically isolated. At the beginning of Egypt's history, natural barriers afforded protection and enabled the country to develop a unique civilization. The distinctive art forms, architecture and religious beliefs had become sufficiently established to be able to absorb outside influences without radically altering their own basic concepts.

From earliest times Egypt remained largely untroubled by frequent incursions or attacks by stronger neighbours. Nubia, situated in approximately the same area as the modern Sudan, lay to the south of Egypt; the Nubians were less dynamic than the early Egyptians and any possible threat was minimized by the Egyptian colonization of this area, giving safe access to the riches of Nubia, especially the gold and hard building stone. So successful was this policy that the Nubians eventually became 'Egyptianized' to such a degree that, much later, 'Egyptian' civilization and traditions were nurtured and preserved in Nubia when Egypt had itself fallen to foreign invaders.

The Mediterranean Sea lay to the north of Egypt. Although this facilitated trade between Egypt and other lands bordering the Sea, until fleets of sufficiently competent ships were developed later, the Mediterranean provided Egypt with an effective protection from her enemies. The Red Sea formed a similar barrier on the east side, while, to the west, separated from the Nile Valley by the desert, lay the land of the Libyans. The early inhabitants of Egypt almost certainly had some contact with these people and a trading relationship continued between them throughout the centuries,

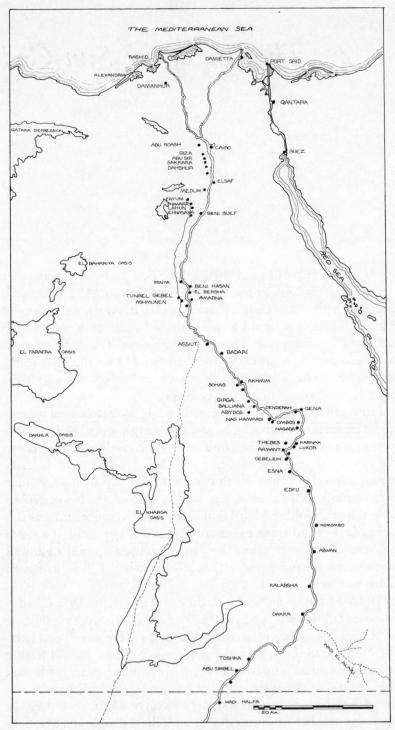

THE MEDITERRANEAN SEA

RASHID　DAMIETTA　PORT SAID

ALEXANDRIA

DAMANHUR

QANTARA

QATARA DEPRESSION

SUEZ

ABU ROASH　CAIRO
GIZA
ABU SIR
SAKKARA
DAHSHUR

EL SAF

MEDUM

FAYUM
HAWARA
LAHUN
EHNASYA　BENI SUEF

EL BAHARIYA OASIS

RED SEA

MINYA　BENI HASAN
EL BERSHA
TUNA EL GEBEL　AMARNA
ASHMUNEN

EL FARAFRA OASIS

ASSIUT

BADARI

SOHAG　AKHMIM

GIRGA
BALLIANA　DENDERAH　QENA
ABYDOS
NAG HAMMADI　OMBOS
NAGADA

DAKHLA OASIS

THEBES　KARNAK
ARMANT　LUXOR
GEBELEIN

ESNA

EDFU

EL KHARGA
OASIS

KOMOMBO

ASWAN

KALABSHA

DAKKA

WADI EL ALAKI

TOSHKA

ABU SIMBEL

WADI HALFA

50 Km.

Map of Egypt

but it was not until a much later period that some of the Libyan tribes and their associates presented a real threat to Egypt's sovereignty. Thus the only relatively easy passage into Egypt was from the north-east, across the northern part of the Sinai Peninsula, and it was probably this route which was used by some of the earliest infiltrators into the Nile Valley.

The earliest inhabitants would have occupied a very different terrain from the Nile Valley of the present day, or, indeed, of the Historic period. During the Palaeolithic period, the Nile Valley was flooded for three months of every year and was covered with lush vegetation for the remaining period. Rushes and papyrus grew profusely and provided shelter for teeming wild life, but prevented man from settling in the Valley. He was forced to live above the valley and occupied the lowest desert spurs which, being more fertile than in later times, became a base for his hunting forays.

Gradually as the valley became drier men began to move down from the desert spurs into this land, rich and fertile from the annual inundation of the Nile. Soon, they began to cultivate the soil and to support themselves more by farming than by hunting. They grew grain, domesticated animals, and, in their newly established groups, presumably devised the rules and customs which became part of their communal existence. They produced domestic articles for daily use, and tools and weapons to assist them in their struggles with the environment. It is in these so-called 'Neolithic' communities that the earliest evidence of religious customs and burial practices becomes available. These cultures continued with little change down to the beginning of the First dynasty which followed the unification of Egypt into one country in c.3100 BC. The span of time in which these communities developed and flourished is generally referred to as the 'Predynastic period'.

Although certain differences are discernible in these communities, and especially between those which developed in Upper Egypt and those in Lower Egypt, it is possible to describe certain features which were common to all. Little is known of the political and social organization, but the dwellings were grouped into village settlements, and each was probably under the direction of its own chieftain. The dwellings were constructed of perishable materials and so little evidence has survived. The community would have been supported by mixed farming, carried out in the

surrounding countryside. Trading contacts were already established between Egypt and other lands and the imports included
ivory from the south, turquoise from Sinai, copper from the north
and shells from the Red Sea or the Persian Gulf.

At some time during the Predynastic period, possibly c.3400
BC, it seems that a new people entered Egypt, to whom scholars
often refer collectively as the 'dynastic race'. Although their existence and entry into Egypt cannot be proven conclusively, it
seems probable that their fusion with the indigenous population
produced the combination of skills necessary to create the
development and technological basis of Egypt's great power.
Some scholars still maintain that this progress can be explained
satisfactorily as a sudden advance by the existing neolithic communities, but a dynamic foreign influence is more likely. For
instance, monumental brick architecture, the sudden appearance
of certain distinctive art forms and script occurred in Egypt at this
period, but archaeological evidence to show that these developed
locally is lacking. It is possible that the newcomers may originally
have had trading contacts with the Egyptians and so came to know
the Nile Valley and to be attracted by its fertile soil. There may have
been a horde invasion, but, more probably, small groups of people
arrived by gradual infiltration. The original homeland of the
newcomers again remains conjectural, although aspects of the
writing and the new architectural and art forms suggest that some
contact existed between them and the developing civilization in
Mesopotamia. Although it may be due to chance or the relative
durability of the writing materials, the cuneiform script found on
mudbrick tablets in Mesopotamia pre-dates any examples of Egyptian hieroglyphic writing. Nevertheless, although there would
appear to be a link between the concept of writing in Mesopotamia
and Egypt, and some underlying principles are common to the
two scripts, once the idea of writing had been received and
accepted in Egypt, a unique script and language developed there.

Another change became apparent at this time, to which we shall
return later; Egyptian burial customs incorporated new features
for the leaders of the communities, including the decoration of the
superstructure of their tombs with recessed brick-panelling,
which also occurs as a feature of the temples in Mesopotamia.
New artistic motifs, often incorporating composite animals with
entwined necks, now appeared on slate palettes produced in
Egypt. Such designs were not Egyptian in origin, but had close

similarites to Mesopotamian motifs. Other artefacts common to both areas included stone maceheads and inscribed cylinder seals.

Although the Mesopotamian connection is usually commented upon, various other places of origin for the dynastic race have been suggested, such as north Syria, Iran, or an as yet undiscovered area or group of areas which could have influenced both the Mesopotamian and, ultimately, the Egyptian forms. Lack of evidence ensures that any reconstruction of events at this period must remain purely speculative.

We do not know how the newcomers entered Egypt; one suggestion is that they used the sea-route, coming via the Red Sea and through the Wadi Hammamat: the great route which lies across the Eastern Desert, linking the Red Sea coast with the Nile Valley. This theory is supported by some archaeological evidence, but a practical aspect is that large numbers of people moving across this desert route would have faced a grave water shortage. Small groups may have survived but it is most unlikely that a horde invasion could have entered Egypt this way. The newcomers using this route would have come first into Upper Egypt and would then have proceeded along the Nile Valley to subjugate Lower Egypt. An alternative route into Lower Egypt would have led them overland from Palestine via the Suez Peninsula into the Delta of Egypt. The invaders probably followed different routes, and some may have entered peacefully while others engaged the indigenous population in combat. The whole process probably lasted for many years, but after the beginning of the First dynasty, there is no further evidence of continuing infiltration into Egypt, and even the architecture and art forms which appear to derive from foreign sources either gradually disappear or become transformed into distinctively Egyptian concepts.

Skeletal remains suggest that the newcomers were of a different race for they possessed larger bodies and wider skulls, and it has been said that this distinct racial type was apparent in the bodies of the nobility who lived in the early dynasties following the unification of Egypt. Indeed, the 'separateness' of the ruling class from the lower classes in Egypt's later history has been explained in terms of an early racial distinction between the conquering newcomers and the indigenous population. This may also have been taken a stage further in the Old Kingdom custom of intermarriage between members of the royal family, which preserved the myth of their divinity, but also continued their separation from the lower classes. Over the years, the two races gradually fused, and from this perhaps came the great advances of the early dynasties.

Little is known of the social and political organization of the newcomers, although they seem to have taken over the pattern of settled communities already in existence. It was perhaps at this period that the separate village communities became organized into larger units. Each district would have had its own chieftain and its own deity, represented in the form of a fetish or an ensign. Gradually, these units were amalgamated into larger groups, which were equivalent to the later 'nomes', or geographical and political divisions of the land. Each would be independent and would have its own capital city, surrounded by land with loosely defined boundaries.

Eventually, these districts divided into two independent kingdoms; one was in the north, based in the Delta and extending perhaps as far as Atfih, with its centre at the king's residence at Pe in the Delta. Nearby was the town of Dep (later known as Buto) where the cobra-goddess Edjo was worshipped. This kingdom was known as the 'Red Land' (not to be confused with the geographical 'Red Land' or desert), and the king wore the Red Crown. In Upper Egypt there was a southern kingdom called the 'White Land' which probably extended from Atfih to Gebel el-Silsileh. The capital was at Nekhen (Hieraconpolis) near Edfu. Here, the king wore the White Crown, and when Egypt was later united under one ruler, he and all subsequent kings of Egypt wore both the Red and White Crowns, either separately or sometimes combined together as the Double Crown. The protective deity of Upper Egypt was the vulture goddess Nekhbet whose centre was at Nekhen. When Egypt was united as one kingdom, the cobra and vulture goddesses of north and south came to be regarded as dual protectors of the king; similarly, the symbols of the Two Lands – the papyrus plant and the bee of Lower Egypt and the sedge of Upper Egypt – became the symbols of the united land of Egypt. The contrast between the old northern and southern kingdoms was retained throughout Egypt's long history, and the people never forgot the dual political origin of their country referring to it as the 'Two Lands'. To some extent, the contrast between Upper and Lower Egypt and their inhabitants is still evident today. Lower Egypt, situated at the cross-roads of ideas and influences from Africa, Asia and Europe, has the two great cosmopolitan cities of Cairo and Alexandria, compared to the mainly agricultural and traditional communities of Upper Egypt. Continuous invasion, infiltration and intermarriage has occurred over the centuries, but it is still possible to recognize two basic racial types in the tall, slender and dark-skinned inhabitants of Upper Egypt, and the shorter, stocky and often lighter-skinned city-dwellers of the north.

An important development occurred at some time during the Predynastic period, which profoundly affected the political organization of the country. This was the artificial irrigation of the Nile Valley. Technological advances enabled the Egyptians to undertake this enterprise, and to be successful, a degree of cooperation was required between the neighbouring communities along the length of the Nile. Perhaps more than any other single factor, this common need united the people of the valley and the Delta. Towards the end of the Predynastic period, the necessary social and political organization and interaction between communities enabled a common irrigation system to be brought into use.

The unification of the two independent kingdoms took place c.3100 BC, when the kings of Upper Egypt and their allies – the chieftains of the area – conquered the kings of Lower Egypt. Archaeological evidence indicates that one of the victorious southern rulers was a King Scorpion, but the final credit for the unification is given to his successor, King Narmer, who became the first king of the First dynasty. A great slate palette was discovered in the temple of Horus at Hieraconpolis (Nekhen) in 1898, which was perhaps dedicated by the king as a thank-offering for his victory over the north. The scenes carved on the palette commemorate the defeat of the north and the subsequent unification of Egypt. The first ruler of the united country moved his capital to a new city in the north which was later known as Memphis; possibly this was considered a safer site from which to rule Egypt and to protect the new state from any uprising in the north. Here, the king identified himself with the god Horus, and was regarded as the earthly embodiment of the god. He bore the title of Horus during his lifetime and handed it on to his successor at death. The queen too had considerable prominence as did the king's mother. This may suggest that the order of succession already passed through the king's principal wife. In later periods, it was maintained that each king of Egypt was the child of the chief state god and the ruling king's Great Royal Wife. Each ruler thus claimed divine conception although he was born to a human royal mother. This enabled him to have a unique relationship with both gods and men. The role of Great Royal Wife – the king's principal queen – was therefore of the utmost importance to the succession. To substantiate his claim to the throne and to ensure the acceptance of his son as heir, the heir to the throne frequently married his own full or half-sister, who, as eldest daughter of the ruling king and queen, was the Great Royal Daughter. She would become the Great Royal Wife and, as divine consort of the god, would eventually become mother of the next king. Whoever married the Great Royal Daughter strengthened his claim to rule Egypt and later, it was not unknown for 'upstart' pharaohs with little claim to the throne, to legitimatize and consolidate their position by marriage to the Great Royal Daughter.

Already in the early dynastic period, it is possible to imagine the kings as absolute monarchs, assisted in their increasing burden of duties by members of the royal family and the nobility. It was from this structure that the elaborate and centralized bureaucracy of the Old Kingdom developed.

We must now consider the development of the religious and funerary customs during the Predynastic period and the early dynastic period, against the background of this social framework. The earliest evidence of a religious awareness in Egypt is found in the first neolithic settlements. Lack of written evidence limits our knowledge of this period, but already the Egyptians displayed great concern for the burial of the dead, and the cemeteries of the Predynastic period provide more information than the corresponding settlements of the living. Objects were buried with the bodies and suggest that, even at this early date, the Egyptians already had a clearly defined concept of continued individual existence after death. The reason behind their veneration for the dead will probably remain uncertain, but they may have believed that the dead continued their link with the living, perhaps providing a bridge between the living and the gods, or they may have feared the revenge of the dead on the living to such an extent that they sought to placate them by giving them elaborate burials. The graves were simple oval or rectangular pits in the sand and were usually only a few feet deep. A small pile of sand or stones was placed on top probably to distinguish it as a place of burial. The grave usually accommodated only one body, although sometimes there were multiple burials. The body lay in a contracted position, usually on its left side, facing west, and was covered by a piece of coarse matting or enclosed in an animal skin or a woven covering of twigs. Even at this stage, the deceased was placed to face the setting sun, although there is no evidence that such a custom was yet associated with sun-worship. The body was adorned with linen clothing, belt and headware, and provided with jewellery, combs and palettes for grinding eye-paint, cosmetics and ivory cosmetic jars, flint tools and pottery, all for use in the next life. Special magical implements were found in the graves of some of the leaders of the communities.

With the advent of the dynastic race, certain changes occurred in the burial customs which may be attributable to the newcomers. Until this time, the chieftain of a village, although he may have possessed a larger grave, had a burial no different to other members of his community. From now on, however, a clear distinction becomes apparent between the burials of the ruling classes and those of the masses. It has been suggested that initially the difference in burial marked not only a social but also a racial distinction. Shallow round or oval graves continued to be used for the burial of the lower classes – descendants of the indigenous population – but more elaborate tombs were introduced for the burial of the new ruling class and their families who were the descendants of the newcomers to Egypt. From these tombs was developed the model which was to continue for many years and which came to be used by all those who could afford its construction. The body was contained in the substructure below ground level, while the super-structure, above ground level, consisted of a series of chambers which contained the burial goods of the deceased. These differed little from the grave goods of the earlier periods, consisting mainly of amulets and beads, stone vessels, tools and small metal articles, mace-heads and decorated pottery. It is uncertain whether the newcomers had introduced the new burial customs from elsewhere or whether they adopted the customs of the older inhabitants, and adapted and improved them for their own use. The burial customs of the two groups appear to merge by the end of the Second dynasty in those areas where fusion of the two races was probably well advanced, and, eventually, during the dynastic period, the continuation of differences in burial customs was a reflection of a man's status and wealth rather than any indication of his specific racial group.

By the First dynasty, the type of tomb which is referred to today by Egyptologists as a 'mastaba tomb' was being used by the ruling classes. The shape of the superstructure of such a tomb resembles the outline of a bench, for which the Arabic word is *mastaba*. This tomb was designed as a house for the deceased and incorporated many of the features of the earlier tombs. Its use continued in later periods, and its basic layout had much in common both with a domestic dwelling and a temple which was regarded as the house of a god.

During the First and Second dynasties, the mastaba tomb went through various stages of architectural development; its design also varied to some extent according to the social status and wealth of its deceased owner. Nevertheless certain basic trends emerged. At first, the mastaba tomb consisted of a substructure, cut into the desert rock, and divided by a series of cross-walls into a number of brick-built chambers. The largest of these formed the burial chamber, while adjoining rooms housed some of the funerary equipment. A brick superstructure, erected at ground level, covered and extended beyond the substructure, and was built as an oblong, rectangular platform. The outer surfaces were faced with recessed brick panelling which imitated the facade of a royal palace of the period. The interior of the superstructure was hollow and part of it was divided into compartments in which subsidiary funerary equipment was stored. The tomb was surrounded by an enclosure wall. Some burials were also provided with a brick-lined boat-pit, situated on the north side, beyond the enclosure wall, and these would have contained wooden boats. Such boat-

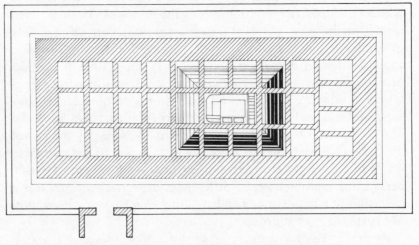

Figure 1 A First dynasty mastaba

burials have been found at Helwan, Saqqara, and Abu Roash, and may indicate the existence of a sun-cult at this early period, for similar boat burials occur later in the Old Kingdom, in association with the pyramids, and were intended to transport the deceased to the sky to join the procession of the sun-god. The earlier boat-burials may, however, have had no connection with a solar cult, and were possibly intended for use by the deceased in his journeys on the river.

Another curious feature of some of these early burials is the existence of subsidiary burials outside the enclosure walls of the tombs. These are arranged in rows running parallel to the sides of the main mastaba, and here, women and members of the deceased's household were buried to serve him in the next world. There is little doubt that these subordinates were buried at the same time as the tomb-owner, for in some cases, the superstructure was erected over the main burial and the subsidiary graves. It is possible that these people took poison, or perhaps allowed themselves to be buried alive at the time of their master's interment. In other complexes, where the subsidiary graves are not included under the main superstructure, the subordinates may have died of natural causes and have been buried near their lord, but on separate occasions. The extent of such human sacrifice at this period is uncertain, but it seems to have continued for longer in the south than in the north, and probably ceased altogether during the Second dynasty.

The elaborate tomb equipment undoubtedly attracted tomb robbers, and the general trend in tomb architecture was to deepen and enlarge the substructure to prevent such intrusions. Changes were gradually introduced during the First dynasty, but could not deter the thieves. Other changes in design included the end to the

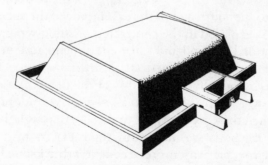

Figure 2 The Mastabat Fara'un

custom of incorporating store-rooms in the superstructure. The funerary furniture was transferred to the burial chamber, and subsidiary rooms were used to store food and drink. The 'palace facade' decoration of the outer walls of the mastaba also disappeared, and the recesses in the panelled facade which had come to represent niches were reduced to two niches positioned at the end of the east face of the mastaba. One represented a subsidiary entrance, and the other a false entrance to the tomb where offerings of food could be placed by the living relatives for the dead man's ka or spirit. This, it was believed, could come forth from the burial chamber to receive the offerings.

Internally, the basic tomb plan was also altered. By the end of the Second dynasty, the tombs of the royal family and the great nobles had become standardized, and although they varied in size and number of chambers according to the status and wealth of the owner, the tombs represented 'houses' and included rooms representing those found in the dwellings of the living. These underground 'houses' included a reception room, on either side of which were guest rooms. The innermost chamber contained the body, and compared with the master's bedroom in a house. There was also a living room, and a harem for the women. In ancient Egypt, the 'harem' was not a place of confinement and seclusion, but provided an area where the women could sit and talk, and follow their own pursuits of weaving and playing with their small children. The burial chamber and the 'harem' both had access to a bathroom and a lavatory. Entry to the tomb was gained by means of a stairway, from which storage magazines led.

The burials of the poorer classes and subordinates followed the old customs. The bodies were still placed in oblong pits, roofed with timber. A low rectangular superstructure with a rounded top was placed over the pit. In the latter part of the period, a false door was cut into the south end of the east facade of the superstructure. The body was placed in the contracted position wrapped in linen and surrounded by food and toilet equipment, and, in the case of many of the artisans, by the tools of their trades.

However, gradually the customs of the upper classes began to drift downwards, and some of the lower classes adopted the new features when they could afford to do so. Although the pit-grave continued, the body was now sometimes placed inside a wooden coffin and the pit was more frequently brick-lined. Probably because of the problem of tomb-robberies the tomb equipment became less lavish, except in the royal tombs, whereas the structure of the tomb gradually became much more elaborate and sophisticated.

Nevertheless this was the period when the pattern for equipping the tomb was established and when the first attempts were made to preserve the lifelike appearance of the body. The basic religious belief, regardless of the status of the deceased, was that life continued after death; this theory apparently existed amongst the neolithic communities of Egypt before the arrival of the dynastic race. Later, the concept varied according to whether an individual was royal, noble or a peasant, but for all classes, there were always two basic requirements – that the body should be preserved in as lifelike a condition as possible, and that the deceased should be provided with equipment for the afterlife. This ranged from the simple possessions placed with a peasant to the elaborate equipment found in the tombs of the kings, queens and great nobles. Such provision included food and drink for the continuing sustenance of the deceased; in some tombs, a complete meal was set out on dishes near the body, outside the coffin. Reserve food supplies were contained in the storage magazines of the tomb, and additional food offerings were brought by relatives and placed in the niches cut into the outer walls of the tombs. Decorated funerary stelae also provided an additional magical food supply.

The other requirements of this life were catered for after death by the supply of furniture, tools and weapons, chests of clothing, jewellery, and games. Thus it was believed that the vital force of the deceased continued to be tied to this world even after death; it could return to the tomb where, through its preserved body, it received sustenance from the food and drink offerings and continued to enjoy the material possessions placed in the tomb.

Central to this belief was the need to preserve the body. Mummification of the dead was unknown as yet, but bodies placed in pit-graves were naturally desiccated; the hot, rainless climate and dryness of the sand around the body produced a rapid process of desiccation and the bodily fluids were absorbed by the porous sand, preventing decomposition of the body tissues. Later, accidental exposure of the body, perhaps by the wind or desert animals, would have made subsequent generations aware of the preservation of their ancestors' bodies. However, with the increased sophistication in building techniques and the lining of

pit-graves with mud-brick or wood, the body was now surrounded not by sand but by the space inside the lined tomb, and
decomposition of the body took place before natural desiccation
could occur. In the Archaic period, there is no evidence of an
attempt to remove the internal organs, to prevent rapid decomposition, and the use of natron as a preservative is only suggested
by one example where corrosion on the bandages next to the skin
indicates that there may have been an attempt to coat the skin
surface with natron. However, the Egyptians of the Archaic
period generally relied on another technique; since the bodies of
royalty and the nobles now decomposed shortly after burial, by
the Second dynasty they had devised a method of reconstructing a
lifelike resemblance to the deceased by moulding the shape and
contours of the living form on the dead body. The linen cloth
which had been wrapped around the body in the Predynastic
period and the First dynasty was replaced by layers of linen pads
and bandages. These were soaked in a resinous substance and
moulded over the body to give a recognizable shape to the face,
torso and limbs. Although the body rapidly decayed within the
wrappings, the padding gave the body a continuing life-like form.
Special attention was given to certain important areas such as the
face, breasts and genitalia, where the details were painted in. The
arms, legs and fingers were individually wrapped. The body was
placed in the burial chamber of the mastaba, either on a bed or in a
wooden coffin. A further precaution was taken, probably only for
royalty, in case the carefully prepared body should not survive to
receive the eternal food offerings; the deceased was provided with
an almost life-size wooden figure of himself which remained in his
tomb with all the other funerary provisions.

Although the lack of written evidence limits our knowledge of
many aspects of the religious beliefs and customs of the Egyptians
during this early period, and although the cemeteries and burial
goods provide us with more information of their funerary practices than of their gods and their worship, it is nevertheless possible to trace something of these other aspects of their religion.

Religion reflected the gradual evolution noticeable in the political and social spheres. In general terms, before Egypt was unified,
each community had its own deity. Political development, with
the amalgamation of villages into larger units, also brought
changes in religion. The deity of an assimilated tribe or village
would be united with that of the victorious community; some of

the conquered deities died out, but others became assistants to the victorious god. The deities of these larger geographical and political units were themselves amalgamated when the communities were organized into nomes, and the god of the most important clan became the god of the whole nome and the protective deity of the nome's chieftain. The nome deities had local influence, over a limited geographical area, although some deities, such as the mother-goddess and her consort, seem to have assumed a considerable and almost national importance.

The grave goods of the neolithic communities indicate that, at this time, great importance was attached to the cult of the cow as supreme mother-goddess. Although we do not know the name of this deity, she was obviously associated with fertility and, through an association with the idea of re-birth after death, she may have acquired a connection with the dead. Her young consort, who was her son and her lover, was probably a later addition to the cult, but he too appears to have had close associations with the fertility of the land, and of its crops and its people. The influence of the goddess in society was probably considerable and was perhaps reflected in the important role which some women seem to have played in these early communities. From the relative size of their burials, and some of the contents of their graves, it would appear that they were powerful and perhaps believed to have special magical powers.

Magic obviously played an important part in the life of the earliest communities, and magical implements were found in the graves of the chieftains. Each leader probably acted as both magician and priest to his community, and after his death he may well have been accredited with special powers which enabled him to contact the gods and the dead, and to transmit renewal of vigour and fertility to the living.

The arrival of the newcomers probably had some effect upon the religious beliefs and customs of the indigenous population, but the degree of that influence is uncertain. It is difficult to determine whether the dynastic race brought in new ideas or whether they adopted existing beliefs and customs and adapted them to their own purposes and needs. Political considerations may have forced the newcomers to tolerate the continuation of the already existing deities, and many tribal, local gods continued to be worshipped as before. As the fusion of the two races progressed, the gods of both peoples probably merged together to form a pantheon which was

mutually acceptable . The local gods were never entirely obliterated, although some of their earliest characteristics may have been
altered or entirely lost. Perhaps only one god, .Seth, who was
probably one of the most powerful of the indigenous deities, was
not assimilated and became an outcast whose followers were
subdued. We shall return in due course to the fate of this god and
the associated myths.

One of the most interesting aspects of early religion is the
existence of an animal cult. In the neolithic communities, the grave
goods indicate that the people revered and worshipped animals.
Not only did they place amulets in the form of animals in the
graves, either to protect the deceased or to supply him with a
source of food in the next world, but animal burials also occur, on
a scale to indicate that they were highly respected. Again, on
decorated pottery found in the graves, some deities are shown in
the form of animals. Indeed, most of the tribal and nome gods
were represented in the form of animals, or trees, or inanimate
objects, and not as humans. A process which may have originated
during the Predynastic period but which is most noticeable in the
Archaic period was the gradual process of anthropomorphization
of most of the local deities who had originally appeared in animal
or inanimate forms. Some deities first acquired a degree of human-
ization in the early dynastic period, when they are shown with
bird or animal heads on human bodies, but by the Second dynasty,
some animal deities possess completely human forms. The Egyptians continued to deify and worship animals on a wide scale
throughout their history, but the reason behind the origin of the
animal cults in uncertain. It may have been because they often
assisted man in his struggle for survival, or perhaps because they
feared them and hoped by worship to placate them and avert their
destructive powers. The animal, as indeed other fetish forms,
probably came to be regarded as a location which the divine power
could inhabit and in which it could be made manifest.

In addition to the original tribal or local gods, there is evidence
that another group of deities existed which we describe today as
'cosmic deities'. Unlike the local gods, they did not possess animal
or fetish forms, but always assumed human characteristics. They
were the great deities of the universe – of the sun, sky, earth and
the elements – and later generations of worshippers apparently
regarded them as unapproachable and awesome because of their
physical distance from men. Their characteristics were quite dif-

ferent from those of local gods – at first, they did not possess cult centres on earth, and they did not originally have physical forms or personalities. They may have been introduced into Egypt by the dynastic race, and eventually, through the gradual process of syncretism, by the Archaic period they became established alongside the local gods and took over some of their cult centres and even some of their physical characteristics and attributes. An alternative explanation is that they had originated in Egypt, existing alongside the tribal deities from earliest times, but worshipped from afar by the local Egyptians. Gradually, they had acquired some of the characteristics of the more approachable local deities, and had taken human forms. Whatever their origin, by the Archaic period their worship was firmly established in Egypt, and they continued to exist side by side with the local gods. Both groups of deities exerted a great influence on the religious beliefs, funerary practices and forms of worship throughout Egypt's history.

The sun-god was himself a cosmic deity. As with so many other aspects of religion in this period, the origin of the solar cult in Egypt remains a matter for speculation. Some scholars believe that a native sun-cult existed whereas others have suggested Arabia, Crete, or Western Asia as its source. Even if the cult of Re, later to be worshipped in Egypt as the sun-god, had been brought in from elsewhere, there may have been an earlier sun-cult already established in Egypt which the followers of Re adopted and absorbed. The symbol of the sun – a circle with a central spot – first appears in the late Predynastic period. Although the cult of the sun only reached prominence in the Old Kingdom (and at one time, it was believed that solar worship was not introduced into Egypt as a state cult until this time) there is evidence that the god was worshipped at least as far back as the earliest dynasties, and perhaps before that, in the predynastic period. We already know that in the early dynastic period there was a custom for burying funerary barques in graves associated with some of the large tombs at Saqqara, Abu Roash and Helwan. This may have been intended to enable the deceased to join the sun-god encircling the heavens in his own solar barque. This was perpetuated in the Old Kingdom, when barques were provided in association with the pyramids for use by the king in his eternal existence accompanying the sun. However, it has already been mentioned that these barques could have been provided for an entirely different purpose in the Archaic period, possibly to enable the deceased to travel by river between the great religious centres of Abydos and Saqqara. Their discovery does not necessarily indicate the presence of a solar cult at this time.

Nevertheless additional evidence of a sun-cult and its growing importance in the Archaic period is provided by the fact that the king is known to have taken 'son of Re' as one of his royal titles in the Second dynasty, and from this time onwards, the sun-god began his close association with the king, and his rise to prominence as the royal god. However, although this relationship was to develop in the later periods, this does not mean that the association existed in early times. The first royal god and protector of the king was a sky-god, shown in the form of a hawk, who became identified with Horus. By the Second dynasty, the sky-god and the sun-god had fused into a deity known as Re-Harakhte. Horus and Re continued to be closely associated with the king, but do not appear to have entered into direct conflict. Both deities were cosmic gods, and their amicable relationship may have stemmed originally from an alliance between the followers of the two gods. If both cults entered Egypt from outside, their supporters may have united in a confrontation against the major deity of the indigenous population.

This deity, it has been suggested, should perhaps be identified with the god who appears in later mythology as Seth. He is represented in Egyptian art as a strange and unidentified species of animal and plays an important role in later mythology. Indeed, the well-known myth of the conflict between Horus and Seth may reflect the political and religious events either of the later predynastic period, following the arrival of the newcomers in Egypt, or of the Second dynasty. Although many of the main elements of this myth can be found scattered throughout Egyptian literature, the complete version of the story has only come down to us through the works of the Greek writer, Plutarch. It tells of a human king, Osiris, who brought civilization and agricultural knowledge to Egypt. He had a brother named Seth who was bitterly jealous of Osiris, and contrived to murder him. When the deed had been carried out, the body of Osiris was dismembered and the parts scattered throughout the major cities and towns of Egypt. Isis, the devoted sister and wife of Osiris, then gathered the parts of her husband's body together again, and posthumously conceived a child by him. This son was named Horus, and he was reared in the marshes of the Delta, away from the wickedness of his uncle Seth. When he was fully grown, Horus wished to avenge his father's death, and set out to fight Seth. The conflict was bloody, and eventually the dispute was brought before a tribunal of gods, who decided in favour of Horus. They restored Osiris to life, resurrecting him not as a king of the living but as a king and judge of the dead in the underworld. They gave the kingship of Egypt to Horus, and condemned Seth as the 'Evil One', who became an outcast.

There are different interpretations of some parts of the myth, but the basic story remains unchanged, perhaps Osiris may have been an early ruler who actually lived and led his followers into Egypt from somewhere in Asia Minor, or even Africa. Plutarch's version may be based on an original account which dated back to the beginnings of Egypt's history. This attempted to represent, in mythological form, the conflicts which arose between the indigenous supporters of Seth, and those groups of newcomers who worshipped and were led by Horus and Osiris, and who perhaps (although no such mention of Re occurs in the myth) were assisted in their struggles by yet another group of newcomers who followed the sun–god Re. The myth discredits Seth as the 'Evil One', but provides good propaganda for Horus, the god of the victorious newcomers. Any reconstruction of political events which is based on such a myth must remain conjectural and indeed some would argue that the events in the myth do not reflect conditions at the end of the Predynastic period, but refer to the political and religious conflicts in the Second dynasty. During this period, Seth still apparently rivalled the position of the royal god Horus, and it was only at the end of the Second dynasty that the conflict between Horus and Seth and their followers was resolved and the supremacy of Horus was established. From then on, Seth was personified in art and literature as an evil god. His cult was apparently irreconcilable with that of Horus and the other major deities. He was cast out and his supporters and their descendants gradually accepted the other gods of the pantheon.

So Horus and Re became important royal gods. By the Old Kingdom, Re had established his cult-centre at Iwnw (later known as Heliopolis) which he had taken over from the earlier god of the centre, Atum, together with some of his attributes. It was here that the Heliopolitan doctrine was developed by the priests of Re, and from this centre, the cult of Re came to influence some of the most important religious aspects of the Old Kingdom.

# 3   The Place of Ascension

The solar cult reached its zenith during the period known as the Old Kingdom; this stretched from the Third to the Sixth dynasties, and was characterized by Egypt's development into a highly organized state which revolved totally around the king. The ruler came to exercise such absolute control over his subjects and resources by the Fourth dynasty that King Cheops was able to divert a large proportion of the manpower and wealth of Egypt towards the task of constructing his great burial complex at Gizeh. Here he built the Great Pyramid and the surrounding tombs of his family and courtiers, and we now turn to the relationship between such pyramid complexes and the sun cult.

The political and social organization of the country also resembled a pyramid shape. At the top, separated from his people by his own divinity, was the god-king. In theory, he owned all the land, its resources and its people, who were entirely subject to his will. However, even the king was inferior to Ma'at, the goddess who personified the concepts of law, justice, and the correct order and balance of things. The king of course delegated some authority and onerous duties to royal officials. The highest posts were usually reserved for immediate members of the royal family, at least in the Fourth dynasty, thus ensuring their loyalty to the king. He also supervised their upbringing and education and they could expect to receive gifts of royal land, and eventually tombs, funerary possessions and endowments to maintain their tombs. Their ultimate ambition was to rest in a tomb, furnished and provisioned by the king, at the foot of the royal pyramid, so securing their eternity through proximity to the king. The vizier held the most important position in Egypt after the king. Usually closely related to the king, he had authority over the organization and administration of the government, and his considerable roles including head of the judiciary, keeper of the state archives and chief royal architect were perhaps designed to fulfil any ambitions which might otherwise have prompted a coup. Nevertheless royal birth was not the only method of self-advancement and able subjects who won the favour of the king through ability could be promoted through the ranks to the highest positions. In particular, the king exercised complete authority over the appointment of local governors to the nomes; these administrative districts were given into the temporary care of loyal subjects who might retain them, subject to the king's wishes, during their lifetimes. The relative geographical isolation of some of these districts from the centralized government could otherwise have encouraged local rebellion by the provincial governor, and indeed, when the positions later became hereditary, disintegration of the system followed.

A sophisticated bureaucratic administration had evolved in Egypt by the Old Kingdom. The treasury, armoury, the granaries, the department of public works, the various priest-hoods of the great temples and the king's burial complex with its mortuary temple and residence city were probably administered from the capital city of Memphis. The army, which was as yet a non-professional body brought together whenever necessary by enforced military service, and trading and diplomatic ventures were also organized centrally. The government departments were housed together with the royal living quarters and the name of 'Great House' was given to this complex of buildings. Later, this name of *per-wer* was applied also to the person of the king, giving us the name 'Pharaoh' for an ancient Egyptian ruler.

Below the ranks of the state officials were the craftsmen whose primary duty was to supply goods of all sorts for the equipment of the tombs of the royal family and the nobility. Obviously many of them would reside at Memphis to carry out their work. In addition to the funerary goods, they also produced articles such as jewellery, furniture and toiletries for the well-to-do. The standards of craftsmanship were very high and later generations of artisans looked to this period for inspiration and example.

At the base of this 'social' pyramid, there were the masses who toiled to work the land whose resources could be used to support the vast funerary complexes of the kings. Although not literally slaves, the lowest classes were nevertheless tied to the land and constant toil for their divine master. They could also be called upon to serve on military expeditions or to work at the quarries or the building sites. Because of the annual inundation when the Nile flooded its banks, the land lay under water and could not be cultivated for three months of the year. During this period, the peasantry were unemployed, threatened with starvation, and a possible threat to the safety and stability of the king and the state, so this surplus manpower was used by the kings of the Old Kingdom to build the pyramids. Whether this was prompted by religious motives or political astuteness, it is impossible to determine. The men were paid in kind and the food thus provided for themselves and their families gave them little choice but to labour annually to complete the final resting-place of the king. However, it is probably unlikely that food was their only incentive to complete the pyramid within the short space of each king's reign. A religious factor was almost certainly present in the belief held at this period that only the king was granted eternal existence. Close members of his family and favoured courtiers and officials could hope for a vicarious eternity through his favour and the closeness of their tombs to his pyramid. The peasants who continued to be buried in the pit-graves at the end of the desert could only hope for eternity by participating in the royal re-birth by building the pyramid. Pyramid-building, initiated for whatever reason, had the effect of uniting Egypt politically, socially and in religious terms. Efficient irrigation of the land, natural resources, the development in arts and crafts, as well as the workforce, were all organized and utilized to one end – the construction of a funerary complex for the god-king, on whom every man, woman and child fastened his slender hope of eternity. Art, crafts such as gold-working, sculpture, wood-carving and stone-masonry, writing and religious practices were all directed to this aim, although offshoots were put to practical, everyday uses. Thus, a country whose geographical layout and fragmented historical origins could have made unification difficult was brought under a firm centralized control. This theocracy was able to develop with little interference from outside. There appears to have been no attempt by outsiders to infiltrate the country after the presumed entry of the dynastic race before the unification. Contacts with other areas were limited to increased trade and diplomatic relations with peoples in Asia Minor whose lands bordered the Mediterranean, and to an expansion of Egyptian power in Nubia to the south. Here, the Egyptians were anxious to obtain trouble-free access to the desirable gold and hard stone found in Nubia. The expertise of Egyptian architects, engineers and craftsmen during this period far surpassed that of neighbouring lands.

The pyramid perhaps typifies the political and religious power wielded by the king. Its primary function was to house his body, his *ka* or spirit and his funerary equipment for use in the next world. In tombs previously constructed, we have seen that the burial place was usually situated in the substructure, while the superstructure contained the tomb. The tomb also served as a place on earth where food and drink could be brought regularly to supply the needs of the *ka*. It provided the deceased with a link between the afterlife, and his earthly existence and former haunts. The superstructure sometimes included the offering place, or, alternatively, it was situated adjacent to the tomb. There was a continuing search to discover new techniques which would provide a safe and secure burial place for the body, and such innovations were first applied to the royal tomb and then to those of the nobles. So, when brick-making and the construction of brick tombs were introduced, these techniques were first used in the royal tomb, and later in the smaller tombs of the nobility. Towards the end of the Archaic period, the stonemasons living and working in the vicinity of Memphis developed more advanced skills. Previously, stone had only been used in isolated instances and no example exists of a complete stone building before the Old Kingdom. It was Imhotep, the architect and vizier of King Zoser, the first ruler of the Third dynasty and founder of the Old Kingdom, who first made use of this material and the skills of the local masons to create a unique and magnificent funerary complex at Saqqara for Zoser. With only a few exceptions, the burial place of the king during the Old Kingdom differed radically in concept and design from the tombs of his subjects, stressing the chasm which now existed between the divine ruler and his people. The pyramid remained a royal form of burial which, in its true form, was never copied by commoners. With its surrounding complex, the pyramid came to combine the features and purposes of the substructure and superstructure of the earlier tombs. These tombs, eventually also constructed of stone instead of brick, continued to be the burial places of the nobility of the Old Kingdom.

Figure 3 The Step Pyramid enclosure at Saqqara

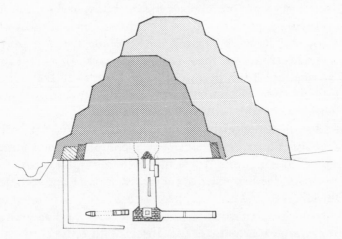

Figure 4 The Step Pyramid, section looking south

The architect of Zoser's pyramid was regarded as a genius by later generations of Egyptians; he was deified in the Twenty-sixth dynasty as the son of the Memphite god Ptah, and he was identified by the Greeks with Asklepios, their god of medicine. From the little information we have, it seems that he was gifted with many abilities – he was a magician, astronomer, founder of medicine, and the vizier, in addition to his most famous role as architect of the first complete stone building which has been discovered – the Step Pyramid at Saqqara. The outer limestone casing of this pyramid has been removed over the years for use as a building material, but the pyramid is still recognizable as a magnificent structure and retains its original form and appearance as it dominates the necropolis at Saqqara. The rest of the surrounding complex, much restored in recent years, can still be seen, and the original grandeur of the site, situated in the desert beyond the cultivation several miles south of Cairo, remains. This first pyramid has as yet preserved its sense of awe, and because of its comparative remoteness, has escaped the modern commercialization of the more famous Gizeh pyramids near Cairo.

The pyramid was probably originally designed as a mastaba tomb, and its final stepped structure has been explained as an attempt to superimpose six mastaba forms, although the reasons behind this idea remain obscure. The burial place was situated in the substructure; a deep shaft gave access to a series of subterranean corridors and chambers where Zoser and members of his family were buried, continuing the practice of earlier rulers who were buried in the substructures of their mastaba tombs.

The pyramid was only the central feature of an entire complex. Walls of white limestone, perhaps intended to represent the brick wall surrounding the king's palace or to simulate the white walls believed to have surrounded the capital city, enclosed the pyramid and the many other buildings in the complex. These included a mortuary temple, shrines, storehouses, altars, courts, gateways and subsidiary tombs. This complex was unique for no earlier example is known and none of the later complexes were as complete as Zoser's which was apparently conceived and executed as a single unit. The buildings show that the architects and artisans lacked previous experience in using stone as a working material on

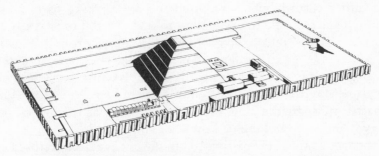

Figure 5 Step Pyramid and enclosure, Saqqara

this scale, and they experimented here with new forms and designs. Some features were now produced in stone which had previously been executed in light wood, reed or brick. The ribbed and fluted stone columns were probably based on the bundles of reeds or palms which had been used as supports in the earlier hut-shrines. Small stone blocks were used here, as an intermediate stage between the brick employed in earlier constructions and the massive stone blocks which the Egyptians handled so confidently in their later buildings. Again, the architects used engaged columns to support the roofs in this complex rather than the free-standing columns of later periods, indicating that they were as yet unsure of their ability to provide sufficient support for the roofs.

Many of the buildings and architectural features occur in pairs, and most of the buildings were designed to imitate brick structures which must have been present in the king's palace complex. Ceremonies carried out during the king's lifetime which were of special importance to the continuing power and efficacy of the kingship were probably also believed to be an essential feature of his afterlife. At Saqqara, areas were provided for their re-enactment in his funerary complex. For example, part of the complex appears to have been connected with the re-enactment of the king's coronation; jubilee festival scenes have been found here, showing Zoser carrying a flail and running around a course. Accommodation for this may have been provided in the oblong court surrounded on its east and west sides by a series of dummy stone chapels. This jubilee festival still remains largely unexplained in terms of its content and purpose, but it probably was enacted at some point during the king's reign to enable him to restore his youth and ability to rule Egypt, by means of magic. It may have been performed on several occasions during his reign, as and when necessary, and was possibly a more civilized version of an earlier custom which required the ageing king to sacrifice himself and to be put to death in some kind of ceremonial ritual, so that he could be replaced by a younger, more vigorous ruler who would revive the strength and potency of the land. The organization of the sacred buildings in the complex into pairs may be explained by the fact that ceremonies here were intended to be enacted twice by the king, once in his capacity as ruler of Upper Egypt and once as king of Lower Egypt.

Today, some of the excavated buildings have been restored by the Egyptian government and they convey something of the

Figure 6 Medum Pyramid

original magnificence of the architecture. This unique complex, with the completeness of its design and the novelty of its building forms and techniques, was never surpassed by later funerary complexes although some of these are better preserved.

Successive rulers followed Zoser's example and built themselves pyramids. Several of these precede the famous group of Fourth dynasty pyramids at Gizeh, and three of them show the stages involved from the building of a step pyramid to the construction of the true pyramid. The Medum pyramid underwent several changes, and was perhaps first conceived as a small step pyramid, before being extended gradually to include seven or eight superimposed steps, and finally transformed into a true pyramid by infilling the steps with local stone and facing the building with a covering of Tura limestone. Of the two other pyramids, both situated at Dahshur, the southern pyramid was planned as a true pyramid, but there was a change in design during the pyramid's construction. About halfway towards the top, the angle of its incline decreases sharply, and its peculiar shape has resulted in the name of the 'Bent' or 'Blunted' pyramid. Perhaps the original angle of its sides may have caused the architects some anxiety and they decided to complete it using a safer angle. The

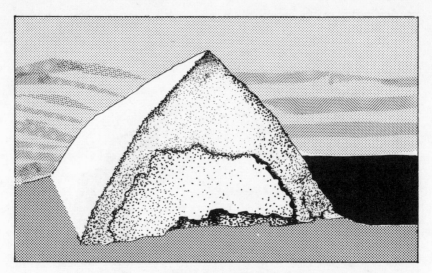

Figure 7 Bent Pyramid, Dahshur

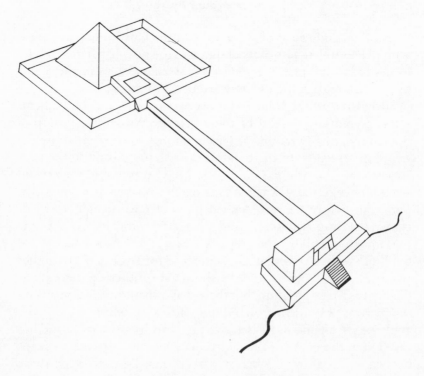

Figure 8 The typical pyramid complex

other pyramid is the first known example of a true pyramid in its complete form.

Pyramid-building reached its zenith with the construction of Cheops' great complex on the Gizeh plateau near Cairo. Gizeh was near to the royal capital and residence at Memphis and there was fine quality limestone in the Tura quarries nearby. Unlike the earlier funerary sites of Abydos and Saqqara, Gizeh was a new site which offered great potential to an imaginative ruler. Here, Cheops could build a funerary structure which would be unrivalled by the tombs or pyramids of earlier kings. He could dominate the new necropolis as he had dominated his court in life. During his reign, as perhaps at no other period, the king was supreme, unchallenged by his nobles, a god to his people. The country was unified and under the absolute control of the god-king; its resources were directed unquestioningly to the construction of a burial-place for the ruler which would be surrounded by the tombs of his family and courtiers, set out at the base of his pyramid to represent in death the organization of the royal court.

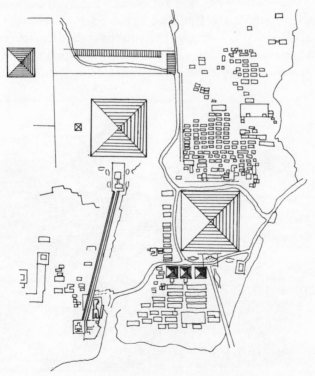

Figure 9 Pyramid complex at Gizeh – plan

His Great Pyramid has aroused interest and speculation amongst writers through the ages; accounts have come down to us from classical authors, Arab travellers, and a succession of European visitors who went to Egypt from the Renaissance period onwards. Various fantastic theories have been put forward to explain its design and purpose, but this massive monument was obviously intended to house the body of the king after death. Changes were made during its construction, but these were mostly internal, and included the replacing of a burial chamber in the rock by one in the body of the pyramid. Hard stone (mainly granite brought from Aswan in the south) was incorporated in the burial chamber and elsewhere, and larger blocks of limestone were used.

Other buildings in Cheops' enclosure have mostly disappeared, providing successive generations of builders with a ready supply of stone. Enough remains, however, to indicate that the complex was organized along the usual lines. A limestone mortuary temple paved with basalt was situated on the east side of the pyramid, facing the Nile, and a causeway led from this temple to the unexcavated Valley Building at the edge of the cultivation. Five boat-shaped pits have also been discovered; three were empty and one has not been excavated, but one pit contained a wooden boat. Such boats may have been connected specifically with the

Figure 10 A reconstruction of the Gizeh necropolis

sun-cult and with the pyramids, but since they also occurred in earlier periods in association with the mastaba tombs, their purpose and origin remains obscure. It is possible that they were carried in the royal funerary procession which led to the pyramid, and were then buried nearby, or they may have been included amongst the funerary trappings so that the dead king could accompany the sun-god on his daily journey across the sky and on his nightly journey through the underworld.

On the plateau to the east of Cheops' pyramid, there are three small pyramids each of which has a small ruined chapel adjoining its east face. One of these is accompanied by a boat-pit, and it has been suggested that this pyramid was the burial place of Cheops' favourite queen. The second and third pyramids have been ascribed to one of the king's daughters and to Queen Henutsen who was possibly his half-sister. However although such subsidiary pyramids have been found in many funerary complexes, their true purpose remains uncertain, for although some may have accommodated the burials of favourite female relatives, others are too small to have contained a full burial and were possibly used for the burial of the king's own viscera or for some other unknown purpose.

To the west and east of Cheops' pyramid lay the fields of mastaba tombs; some were allotted to special members of his family and some were owned by his most influential courtiers and officials. This complex, with Cheops' pyramid towering over the comparatively insignificant mastaba tombs set out in neat, regular rows, dramatically illustrates Egypt's social and political system

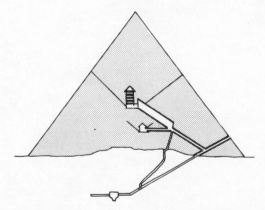

Figure 11 The Great Pyramid, section looking west

during the Old Kingdom. The titles of the men and women who were buried here provide useful information regarding the administration, temple services and court organization of the period, and it is apparent that the cults of Re at Heliopolis and of Ptah at Memphis were of great importance.

However, this great funerary complex, unique in the vastness and orderliness of its conception, was never completed. It presented the same problems of maintenance and supply as a town of the living, and it was a considerable economic drain on Egypt's resources. Not only did the king's daily supply of food and drink, to sustain his spirit after death, require attention, but also his bounty extended to the daily provisioning of the tombs of his family and courtiers. In front of the funerary area proper, land was set aside for the Pyramid City where funerary priests lived who attended to the presentation of funerary provisions and to the recitation of the formulae in the royal mortuary temple. Exempt from taxation, these men and their families were supported by royal endowments of agricultural land.

However, it is the pyramid complex of Cheops' son, Chephren, which provides us with the most complete example of such a funerary area. He built the second pyramid in the Gizeh group. It lies between his father's pyramid and that of Mycerinus, and the three pyramids were built on a roughly diagonal line which runs from north-east to south-west. He did not attempt to copy the

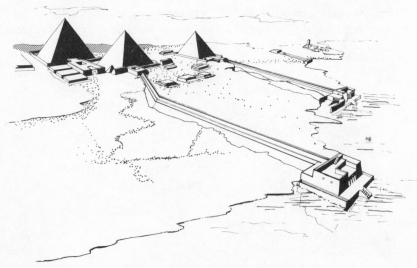

Figure 12 Pyramids at Abusir

1 Scene of cultivation and desert

2 Wooden boat burial, Gizeh

3 Pyramids at Gizeh (group)

4 Great Sphinx at Gizeh

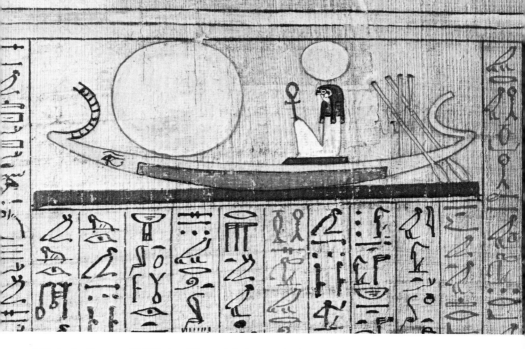

5 Re in the Barque of Millions of Years. Theban *Book of the Dead*. Papyrus of Ani. British Museum

6 Canopic jar with stopper in
form of demi-god

7 Valley Building of Chephren, Gizeh

8 Temple of Karnak – Hypostyle Hall

9 Stone relief of Amen-Re
embracing the Egyptian ruler

10 Obelisks in Temple of Karnak

11 A temple ritual wall scene,
showing king offering to a god

12 Pyramid texts on walls in Pyramid of Unas, Saqqara

family cemetery of Cheops, and his queens and children were buried in rock-cut tombs to the east of his pyramid, south of its causeway. Nevertheless this is the first fully developed pyramid complex on which all such complexes were later based. It is the best preserved in outline, and still retains some of its outer lime-stone casing.

The pyramid itself was the main element in a series of adjacent buildings connected with ceremonies which ensured the king's ascent to heaven. To reach this desired state of eternal bliss, the correct rituals had to be performed at the time of burial, and food-offerings had to be presented in perpetuity to sustain the king's spirit. In these corridors, chambers, and rooms, it is possible to reconstruct the ritual which was probably carried out here at the time of the king's death. Each pyramid was built on the edge of the desert and a causeway joined the pyramid and its adjacent mortu-ary temple to the valley building or temple, built at the edge of the river. The funerary procession and subsequent food supplies could be transported to the complex by river, transferred to the valley building, and taken along the causeway to the mortuary temple and the pyramid. The ritual purpose of the Valley Temple is uncertain, although it obviously played an important part in the funerary ceremonies, as the first area of the complex into which the king's body would be brought. One theory is that the embalm-ing and purification rites were carried out in this building, but another maintains that only a ritual enactment was performed in the Valley Temple, and that the actual processes of mummifica-tion and purification were completed in brick buildings nearby. Purification involved the washing of the king's body to simulate the daily rising of the sun from the water at dawn and the resus-citation of Osiris, and was thought to assist the king's own resurrection. Finally, the Opening of the Mouth Ceremony was performed on the body or on a substitute statue. This ceremony, which also came to be used on the mummies of non-royal persons and which will be discussed later, involved various rites in which the body was sprinkled with water, perfumed with incense, and touched on the mouth and elsewhere with various instruments. The life-giving force was thought to be restored to the deceased's body so that it once again possessed the faculties of a living person. The *ka* or spirit of the deceased was now able to enter the body or statue and receive its sustenance from the food-offerings. The twenty-three statues of the king placed around the T-shaped entrance hall of Chephren's Valley Temple may have been ritually awakened in this manner at the time of his funeral.

Once the preliminaries were completed, and the king's body had undergone the performance necessary for his re-birth, the procession of priests, with their shaven heads and white linen garments, would have escorted the king's body, placed in its coffin and drawn on a sledge, along the passage which joined the Valley Temple to the causeway, and then along the causeway to the Mortuary Temple. The procession would probably have moved to the accompaniment of chanting, and the wafting of incense. Only the flare of the torches lit the king's last journey to his burial chamber. This dark corridor was roofed and enclosed to protect the king's body from the gaze of all except his mortuary priests and to ensure that the ritually-pure mummy of the king was not defiled in any way by contact with the outer world.

This causeway gave access to the mortuary temple which had five main areas – the entrance hall, an open court, five niches for statues, magazines and a sanctuary. This was the place where, after his death, food-offerings continued to be presented to the king's spirit by his staff of mortuary priests. These daily supplies were placed by the priests on a low altar before a false door in the west wall of the sanctuary through which the king's *ka* should pass to receive the offerings. Reserve supplies of food and stone vases were stored in the magazines. Although it played a continuing and important role as an offering chapel, the mortuary temple was also an essential feature of the actual burial rites. Here, it is believed, two sets of ancient burial rites associated with the cities of Buto and Sais were performed. Then the funerary procession passed into the burial chamber, hidden deep within the pyramid, where the king's body was finally placed to rest in a massive sarcophagus. Thus, a ritually pure unit was provided in which the king's body could receive final sanctification and in which it could be conveyed from the river to the interior of the pyramid. Only the priests, who were ritually pure, could pass this way. Access to the pyramid for others, such as the workmen who were on hand to complete and maintain the structure, was provided by a ramp which by-passed the mortuary temple but led to the terrace on which the pyramid was built.

An unusual feature associated with Chephren's pyramid but apparently not found in other complexes is the Great Sphinx. it was carved from a natural outcrop of rock and still dominates the foreground of the Gizeh plateau. The crouching body of a lion supports a human head, whose face, now much damaged, is believed to represent Chephren himself. The reason for its inclusion in this complex is unknown. It may have been regarded as a guardian of the area and was also possibly connected with the sun-cult. Whatever its origin, the sphinx has exerted its fascination over generations of visitors to the site, including the prince who became King Tuthmosis IV of the Eighteenth dynasty. In the so-called Dream Stela, he recounts how he had the sand cleared away from the sphinx and built a temple between its paws, as the result of a dream in which the sphinx communicated with him.

The complex built for Mycerinus completes the group of Gizeh pyramids. According to the literature of the later periods, he was a good and pious king, who did not possess the tyrannical disposition attributed to both Cheops and Chephren. Future kings built their tombs elsewhere, and although pyramid-building continued during the next couple of dynasties and was revived by the kings of the Middle Kingdom, the magnificence of the Gizeh pyramids was never again equalled. The Fourth dynasty was characterized by political and economic conditions which encouraged pyramid-building, and we must now pause to consider the reasons behind the construction of the pyramid as a place of burial, and also the possible relationship between the pyramid and the increasingly powerful cult of the sun.

We have seen that, at some stage in their early history, the Egyptians developed a belief in an afterlife. Although several different concepts of eternity were to emerge, the earliest apparently centred around the continued existence of the individual within the tomb, assisted by the preservation of the body and a constant supply of food, drink and other requirements to sustain the spirit. As well as being regarded as the eternal house of the deceased, the tomb may also have represented a means of entry into the underworld.

The two other important and widespread concepts of eternity were both connected with the worship of a god. The Osirian theory was based on the worship of Osiris, the ancient god of vegetation. At first, this belief was applied only to the king and to his afterlife, but by the Middle Kingdom, the nobility and even the ordinary people identified themselves with Osiris and hope of individual resurrection after death became widespread. The general appeal of this cult soon surpassed the influence exerted by Re, the sun-god, who remained a royal god, and the rise of Osiris was one of the main developments of the Middle Kingdom. Osiris came to be worshipped at all levels of society, whereas Re remained exclusively a royal god, and the afterlife associated with the sun-cult was only obtainable by the king. The two gods had very different roles – Re was a god of the living, whereas Osiris was both a vegetation god and the king and judge of the dead who inhabited the underworld. Although the cults were so different, and the gods presumably had distinct origins, both beliefs had an underlying similarity since they both offered survival after death. In the sun-cult, the sun was re-born daily after the night, and in the Osirian myth there was the annual death and re-birth of the vegetation after the inundation, and the related death and resurrection of Osiris. An association between immortality and natural cycles underlies both cults and this may explain why many elements in the cults could be linked together and why there is very little evidence of direct conflict between the two cults.

We know that the earliest communities worshipped their local tribal deities and that these were eventually amalgamated into an all-embracing and often confusing pantheon, giving the impression that homage was paid to a multitude of gods. Despite this amalgamation of gods at a state level, the individual probably still worshipped only his local god or group of deities. It was during the Old Kingdom that the priesthood attempted to organize and rationalize this confusing assortment of deities by grouping them either into small family units or groups of eight deities (called *ogdoads*) or nine deities (called *enneads*), which were closely associated with specific cult centres. The most important of these theological 'colleges' was based around the cult of Re at On (later known as Heliopolis). Here, in the area which is today a suburb of Cairo, the official solar cult developed in the Old Kingdom. Re absorbed some of the attributes and characteristics of Atum, the deity who was originally worshipped at On or Iwnw, and from this time onwards, we can trace the rise to power of the sun-god Re-Atum who became the foremost deity of the later Old Kingdom. In the temple at Heliopolis, an early fetish existed from which developed the sacred symbol of the sun-god. This probably took the form of a conically-shaped stone and was known as the Benben. This stone may have been regarded as the place of creation – the primeval mound – on which the sun-god settled in the form of a bird. During the Old Kingdom, different theologies

Figure 13 Re-Harakhte

developed at the various cult centres; each one involving a particular group of divinities who were associated with an important city. Each city had a powerful priesthood which co-ordinated the local gods and promoted a theology which related them to the creation of the universe, the gods and mankind. Thus several rival cosmogonies or creation myths grew up, each stressing the importance of a particular group of deities. The most famous of these was the Heliopolitan system which centred around a local family of gods and emphasized the all-powerful creative role of Re-Atum. We shall now turn to this creation myth and the other rival cosmogonies.

An important aspect of the solar theology in relation to the building of pyramids was the concept of the sky and earth, and the role played by the sun-god in connection with the king's afterlife. We have seen that the sun and the Nile were regarded as essential elements in producing the physical conditions of life to which the Egyptians were accustomed and many myths grew up around them. It was believed that the surface of the earth was flat and that it formed the back of the god Geb. He lay in the centre of a circular ocean, the lower half of which flowed through the underworld (the abode of the dead), while the upper half became the sky. The sun was transported across the sky in a boat or barque every day, and at nightfall, passed into the underworld where he changed to his night barque. The cycle was completed when the sun appeared on the earth's surface at dawn the following day. The sky was also personified as the goddess Nut who was sometimes shown as a cow standing over the earth, or as a woman whose bending body formed the sky. She was believed to swallow the sun through her mouth (which was on a level with the western horizon) every evening. It then passed through the length of her body at night, to re-emerge from her at the eastern horizon each morning. It was an important aspect of the sun-cult that the king alone was believed to have access to the next world; his family and favoured courtiers enjoyed a vicarious measure of eternity only because of their proximity to the king in death. This royal eternity was believed to be enjoyed in the heavens to the east, where the king was greeted by the gods and became one of them. As in life, the king continued his royal duties and sat in judgment and also accompanied the sun-god on his daily journey across the heavens in his barque. To reach the gates of the other world the king had to cross a lake which extended from the northern to the southern horizon and use various methods to persuade the ferryman to transport him across this lake.

Although it is generally accepted that the main purpose of the pyramid was to provide the king, and perhaps sometimes also the queens, with a burial place, some architectural and some mythological ideas have been suggested to explain its unique structure. Could the pyramid be the ultimate development of the mound of sand which was piled above a predynastic pit-grave to mark its existence? This may have been explained in mythological terms as the mound or 'Island of Creation' which arose from the state of chaos which existed during the creation of the universe. A direct line of architectural development can be traced from this pile of sand to the superstructure of the solid brick mastaba tomb, through to the stone step pyramid and eventually to the true pyramid. Such a progression is supported by archaeological evidence, for the original mound was included in the early mastaba superstructure. The mastaba form can be seen in the step pyramid structure which is essentially a series of superimposed mastaba forms of decreasing size, and the step pyramid form was incorporated in the true pyramid form.

The concept of a pyramid as a royal burial site may also have resulted from the architect's desire to build a structure which would symbolize the king's superiority over his subjects at this period. Or he may have wished to provide a more secure resting place for the royal body and funerary goods by making the burial chamber, concealed within four sloping walls and with its entrance unmarked, more difficult for the tomb-robbers to penetrate.

The Greeks gave the name *pyramis* to such a structure; it has been suggested that they may have used this word, meaning 'wheaten cakes', because the Gizeh pyramids, stretched out along the distant horizon, had the appearance of small conical loaves or cakes. The word 'pyramid' is probably derived from the Greek. The Egyptians themselves used the word *Mer* to describe these buildings, and its tentative translation as 'Place of Ascension' perhaps provides the real clue to their meaning.

After death the king would pass from earth to heaven, to take his place amongst the gods and to join the retinue of the sun-god. However, he needed a way of reaching the sky from the earth, a bridge slung between this world and the next, a 'Place of Ascension'. The true pyramid form could have been developed at the same time as the rise of the sun-cult to provide this means of ascent, and in the Pyramid Texts of the Old Kingdom, which were intended to aid the king's passage to the next world, certain spells refer to a 'staircase . . . provided for the king's ascent to heaven'.

Other sources tell us that the principles of Egyptian magic included the belief that the replica of an object became endowed with the same properties and qualities as the original. One example was the inclusion of a statue or likeness of a person, carefully named, within a tomb; this was thought to replace that person for the purpose of receiving the food offerings after death. In the same way, it has been suggested that the Egyptians may have created the pyramid form, in gleaming white stone, to reproduce the rays of the sun shining through the clouds. The king's body, buried in this pyramid, was thus enfolded in the sun's rays and could be transmitted to the heavens where he would pass his solar eternity. By the same means, he would be able to return to earth whenever he wished, to receive the food offerings made to his spirit in the mortuary temple. The pyramid burial place would thus have played an essential role in a royal afterlife which was so closely linked to the sun-cult.

We have seen that the true pyramid was the culmination of several unsuccessful attempts to develop the step pyramid. It is possible that the physical progression from step pyramids to true pyramids reflected the triumph of the sun-cult over an earlier star-cult which was perhaps associated with the step pyramid. Both types of pyramid may have been intended to provide a magical means of access to heaven. Some literary and archaeological evidence supports this theory. There is evidence that certain spells in the Pyramid Texts relating to stars have a different religious origin from those associated with the solar cult. The step pyramid form was incorporated within the true pyramid and this may have been due to earlier religious elements being absorbed into the solar cult. The mortuary temple was situated on the north side in the earlier complexes, but was placed on the east side of the true pyramids facing the rising sun. If a close association between the royal burial place and the state solar cult is accepted, the funerary complexes of the Old Kingdom which do not conform may perhaps be regarded as attempts by some rulers to turn away from the increasing power of Re and the Heliopolitan priesthood, and perhaps to establish an alternative state cult or revive an earlier cult. The most notable example is provided by the tomb of Shepseskaf, who succeeded Mycerinus as ruler. Built towards the end of the Fourth dynasty, and situated between Dahshur and Saqqara, the tomb was not a pyramid and shows a marked break with the tradition of great pyramid construction at Gizeh. This building was erected as a mastaba tomb, in the form of a large rectangular sarcophagus on a low platform. A small mortuary temple was built on the east side, with a causeway running down to the valley building. The tomb is known today as the Mastabat Fara'un. Khentkaues, who was probably the wife of Shepseskaf, is thought to have erected a similar building at Gizeh, constructed between the causeways attached to the pyramids of Chephren and Mycerinus. The two funerary complexes belonging to Djedefre and Nebka may also have had associations with a cult other than the state solar cult.

Thus the exact interpretation of the pyramid and its association with the state solar cult remains uncertain. We can only deduce that, in architectural terms, there appears to have been a direct development from the earliest graves with their superimposed mounds to the true pyramid form, and that, in religious terms, the pyramid was the royal place of burial, protecting the king's body and his funerary possessions. It may also have been regarded as a means for the king to reach heaven. As such, it would have played a vital role, for the importance of the king's divinity and his successful ascent to heaven after death were central features of Egyptian religion. It is likely that there was a close association between the development of the pyramid form and the growth of the solar cult, with its unique royal afterlife, and that this cult and the true pyramid form superseded earlier cults, including a stellar cult associated with the step pyramid form.

Apart from the magnitude of the pyramid complexes, it is difficult to comprehend the impetus which enabled these buildings to be constructed. Political expediency may have encouraged the rulers to introduce pyramid building as a means of providing the mass of people with work and food during the months of the flooding to prevent the dangers of a large, unemployed, and dissatisfied work-force. Such social and economic factors may well have played a part, but the greatest spur to the serfs to complete at least one of these complexes during the length of one king's reign must surely have been a religious one. At this period, the serfs, together with the rest of society, could only expect a chance of eternity through the successful burial and ascension of their god-king, and their only way of contributing to this was through their labours at his eventual burial place. We shall probably never know the extent to which each of these factors was responsible for the introduction of pyramid-building in Egypt at the beginning of the Old Kingdom, but the results were obvious. In religious, social and economic terms, pyramid-building bound together scattered and isolated communities whose geographical distribution created problems in terms of national unity. This communal purpose created an unprecedented awareness amongst his subjects of the absolute power of their god-ruler and his ability to promote their well-being both in life and after death.

# 4  Mansions of the Gods

The cult of Re achieved such importance during the Old Kingdom that even the monarchy came directly under its spell. In the Fourth dynasty, pyramid-building, which was probably closely linked with solar worship, became the most important single activity of the country, and the priesthood of Re began to wield unprecedented power. The threat of this growing influence may have prompted Shepseskaf, son of Mycerinus, to attempt a break with the solar tradition towards the end of the Fourth dynasty, to abandon Gizeh as the royal burial site and to choose a tomb of a different design. Also, his names and titles had no association with the cult of Re; one of his sons held the high-priesthood of the god Ptah, and it is possible that he elevated the cult of this god, who was the ancient deity of Memphis, above the solar cult, for it would have posed far less of a threat to the stability and power of the monarchy.

However, if he did make such an attempt to diminish the solar cult and to restore royal supremacy, it was short-lived and unsuccessful. His successors – the kings of the Fifth dynasty – not only re-established the importance of the solar cult but gave it such prominence that it eclipsed the monarchy and reduced the status of the king. The background to these events is preserved by a folk-version in the Westcar Papyrus. It was probably invented by the solar priesthood as propaganda to justify the elevated status of their cult and to add credibility to the kings of the new dynasty; it certainly shows considerable royal support for the cult. The story describes how the first rulers of the dynasty were the children of Re himself, born to the wife of a priest of Re, underlining their divinity and unalienable right to rule Egypt, and also their close connections with the sun-cult. We shall see how the tale differs, at least in detail, from the known sequence of historical events.

There is no evidence to suggest that the kings of the Fifth dynasty were born to the wife of an ordinary priest. Indeed, there are no indications that any great upheaval or religious revolution occurred between the end of the Fourth dynasty and the beginning of the Fifth. The kingdom merely seems to have passed from the main branch to a secondary branch of King Cheops' family. Userkaf, the first king of the Fifth dynasty, was probably the son of Neferhetepes who was the daughter of King Redjedef, a descendant of Cheops who built the Great Pyramid at Gizeh. Userkaf married Khentkaues, the daughter of Mycerinus and a sister of Shepseskaf, who represented the main branch of Cheops' family and thus strengthened Userkaf's claim to the thone. Khentkaues played an important although obscure role in the transfer of power from one dynasty to the next. Her religious inclinations are also uncertain, for although the sun-cult was fully restored during the reigns of her husband and of her descendants, Khentkaues was not herself buried in a pyramid but had a tomb in the shape of a sarcophagus which resembled that of her brother, Shepseskaf. The political and religious significance of these facts remains vague, but it is clear that the position of the king and his relationship with the priesthood of Re were fundamentally changed under the new dynasty. The short-lived supremacy of Ptah as royal god was quickly forgotten, although Ptah continued as an important but politically uninfluential deity.

The kings had for some time incorporated the epithet 'son of Re' in their titulary, but this now became regular practice and, perhaps more than ever, reflects the king's new position in relation to the gods. He is now no longer one of the gods, but has entered a filial and subordinate position to the official state-god and his priesthood. Other evidence, such as the record given on the Palermo Stone that temple building and endowment particularly favoured Re, shows that the solar priesthood had become increasingly powerful, while the king and the royal family continued to decline in importance. Gradually, senior administrative posts were no longer filled exclusively from the ranks of the royal family, and the civil service became increasingly independent of the king's favour.

The most tangible proof of Re's power is provided by the series of special sun-temples dedicated to Re which were based on the design of his main temple at the cult-centre of Heliopolis. The first of these temples was built by Userkaf and inscriptions confirm that at least six rulers of the Fifth dynasty put up such buildings, although only two – belonging to Userkaf and Niuserre – have so far been discovered and excavated. The sun-temples were quite separate in concept from the pyramids and adjoining funerary complexes. The kings of this dynasty revived the tradition of pyramid-building along the same lines as those of the Fourth dynasty, although they show a considerable deterioration in standards of workmanship. The pyramids of Sahure, Neferirkare, Neferefre and Niuserre were built at a new royal cemetery at Abusir, but the sun-temples were built at the edge of the desert plateau to the north of Memphis, near the modern village of Abu Gurob.

As the burial places of the kings declined in splendour so the new sun-temples flourished and the solar cult increased its influence. The construction of such temples may have required a smaller workforce than that of the pyramids, but it still imposed a great strain on the country's resources, for not only did the king maintain his own sun-temple but he was also expected to care for and provision the temples built by his predecessors. The cumulative pressures must have been considerable, and, as the sun-cult waned in importance, the construction of these temples ended and they remain a unique feature of the Fifth dynasty.

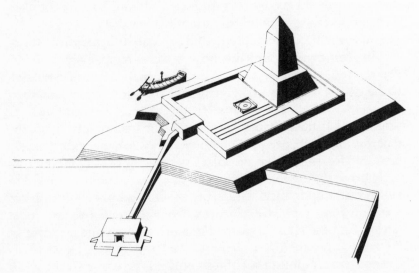

Figure 14 The Sun-Temple of Niuserre

The rise of the solar cult at the expense of the king had originated with the king's own generosity; he had directed vast wealth
in terms of land and resources to the god's cult and in doing so, had
jeopardized the security of the monarchy. The king faced a
dilemma, for as the agent and protector of the gods, he was
obliged to bestow his bounty on them in return for their multitude
of blessings, but this ultimately resulted in the god's power, vested
in his priests, rivalling the supremacy of the king. This situation
first occurred in the Fifth dynasty, but it was a dilemma which was
to be repeated in later dynasties with equally disastrous results.

We should now look at the general design and purpose of these
sun-temples, and the differences in plan and concept between the
traditional temple and the sun-temple of the Fifth dynasty.

Worship of the gods had existed in Egypt from earliest times
and certainly pre-dated the establishment of the traditional temple
building as a place of communion with the deity. In the Predynastic communities, local gods had been provided with reed hut-
shrines constructed of reed-matting and wood which were only
slighter superior to the surrounding dwellings of the worshippers
and their chieftain. An early ebony tablet shows a copy of such a
shrine dedicated to the goddess Neith. The hut stood at the rear of
a small enclosure, fenced around to include a small forecourt
where the symbols of the god were set up and the entrance marked
by two flag-poles. The cult-statue was hidden from public gaze in
the reed hut and was probably the central feature of a simple ritual.
We know nothing of the form of this worship, but the Egyptians
were an extremely conservative race and since the main features of
the hut-shrine and its enclosure were retained in the later elaborate
stone temples, we might assume that the rituals were similar and
consisted of the presentation of food and other offerings to the
cult-statue.

The early tribal chieftain gradually gained more power and the
shrine of the local deity was embellished and improved accord-
ingly. Ultimately, the strongest of these local rulers would seize
power and make himself king of a united Egypt. The deity of his
tribe, and the gods and goddesses of his allies, and even of his
enemies, were eventually amalgamated to form the pantheon. The
god of the victorious tribe was elevated to a position of great
importance in the State. As building techniques became more
advanced, the reed shrines were eventually transformed into magnificent stone temples, intended, like the tombs, to last for ever

unlike the houses and even the palaces which were constructed of mud brick. These temples were known, appropriately, as 'Houses of Eternity'.

Two main types of temple developed from the early reed shrines, but they had little in common with the solar temples of the Fifth dynasty and are known today as 'cultus temples' and 'mortuary temples'. The cultus temple was designed to house the statue of the god, as the earliest shrines had done, and to provide a centre where worship rituals could be carried out. The mortuary temple had originally been attached to the king's pyramid and had been a place where food offerings could be made to the deceased ruler. However, by the New Kingdom, the kings were no longer buried in pyramids but in rock-cut tombs in the famous Valley of the Kings at Thebes. The pyramids had been built at the edge of the desert, with ample space to accommodate the necessary temples and buildings which made up the complex, but the Valley of the Kings is narrow, barren and enclosed. It was hoped that such a place might deter the robbers from ransacking and plundering the tombs of the kings. There was no room here to build mortuary temples or offering chapels and therefore, from the reign of King Amenophis I onwards, the king's tomb and his mortuary temple were physically separate. Most of the mortuary temples of the kings buried in the Valley of the Kings were strung out across the wide, flat plain which lay between the cliffs and the river.

The mortuary temple was intended for the worship of the dead, deified ruler who had built it. However, it could be used for this purpose even when that king was still alive, resulting in the king making offerings to his own future deified and dead form. Mortuary temples could also be dedicated to the chief god of the locality, in which case, both the god's cult and the cult for the dead king would be performed inside the temple. Although their uses were distinct, the cultus and the mortuary temples were indisputably linked and had developed from the same early reed shrines.

Our knowledge of the construction and appearance of the early temples is limited to pictures of the reed shrines and to the existence of the mortuary temples attached to the pyramids of the Old and Middle Kingdoms. Other examples of temples of this type are non-existent during the Old Kingdom. They are sparsely represented in the Middle Kingdom by the Twelfth dynasty temple at Tod which is incorporated into a later Graeco-Roman building, by a chapel at Medinet Maadi and by the most completely

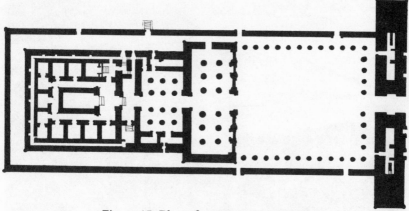

Figure 15  Plan of an Egyptian Temple

preserved temple at Medamud. Temples of this period were undoubtedly used as sources of building material by later generations
and therefore it is from the New Kingdom that most examples of
this type of temple date. The Egyptians were now the proud rulers
of an Empire which encompassed Nubia in the south and many
areas of Asia Minor in the north. Booty brought back by the
military campaigns of the Eighteenth dynasty belonged to
Pharaoh, and the kings once again contributed to their own
downfall by presenting this vast wealth to the temples of the gods
in the hope of obtaining divine blessing and bounty for all Egyptians. Eventually the priesthoods, especially that of Amen-Re,
became so powerful that they threatened the position of their royal
benefactor. Nevertheless such wealth enabled the temples erected
to glorify the gods during the New Kingdom to be magnificent
and awe-inspiring.

All these temples had certain architectural features in common;
the basic layout differing only in detail. The design of the early
reed shrines was preserved to a remarkable degree in these stone
temples. Each rectangular temple was enclosed inside a mud-brick
wall, which protected the sacred building from the gaze of the
townspeople. Today, when one visits these half-ruined buildings,
now often isolated on the edge of the cultivation, it is easy to forget
that they once stood, both physically and emotionally, at the very
centre of the community. A great gateway, flanked by two stone
towers or pylons, stood at the front of each temple. These grand
and statuesque towers had developed from those of woven reeds
which marked the entrance to the enclosure of the reed shrine. The

Figure 16 Roof view of Temple (Edfu)

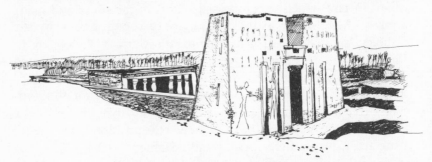

Figure 17 Temple of Edfu

gateway gave access to one or sometimes two colonnaded court-yards. The interior walls were decorated with scenes depicting the activities of the king which found favour with the gods – his prowess in battle against foreign enemies and his filial relationship with the deities who granted him the right to rule Egypt. It is possible that these open areas were the one part of the temple building which ordinary people were allowed to enter, perhaps to make offerings to the resident god and to pray to him, or to participate in his festival by cheering and clapping. However, even this limited degree of access is uncertain and the whole of the temple interior including the courts may have been completely out of bounds to the populace.

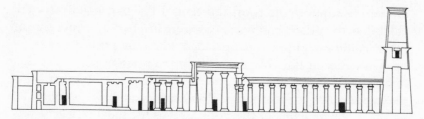

Figure 18 Section of an Egyptian Temple

The courtyards like the open enclosure in front of the reed shrine led to the most sacred, roofed area of the temple. The priestly processions would have followed the main route, leading through the great gateway, across the centre of the courtyards, through the main doorway of the temple proper into the hypostyle halls which lay beyond. Passing from the brilliant sunlight of the courtyards, the priests would have been plunged into the gloom of the hypostyle halls; there were one or two such halls, roofed and dark, lit only with clerestory lighting. Heavy stone columns were massed together, with papyriform and lotiform

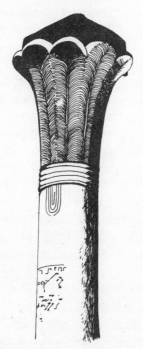

Figure 19 Palmiform capital

Figure 20 Lotiform capital

capitals to support the roof; the central rows of columns were taller than the others and windows were inserted on either side of these. Additional light was provided when the great doors were opened to admit the processions, and the priests themselves carried torches during the performance of the rituals. Nevertheless the hypostyle halls were dark and awesome and this was enhanced by the gradual incline of the floor level as the sanctuary area was approached. This lay at the rear of the hypostyle hall on the main axis of the temple. In the most sacred area of the temple the shrine of the god, which housed his cult-statue, was kept; here, the very essence of divinity was thought to be present and this was where god could be approached by man.

The sanctuary was rectangular, small and dark and had evolved from the reed shrine. Most temples had only one resident deity, although other members of his family were also sometimes present; at the temple of King Sethos I at Abydos, sanctuaries could accommodate six major deities. The sanctuary of the chief god would always be on the temple's main axis, with the sanctuaries of the lesser deities on either side. In some temples, provision was made to house not only the permanent cult-statue but also the god's barque and his lighter, portable statue which would be placed inside the barque and carried around outside the temple during the great festivals.

The god had many possessions which played a vital role in the daily ritual; his clothing, jewellery and insignia were kept in the storerooms surrounding the sanctuary, and other rooms were devoted to various aspects of temple administration. Everything inside the temple was regarded as 'pure' because it came into contact, however indirectly, with the god; therefore, all other activities, such as butchering and food-preparation, were carried out in service areas usually situated outside the temple but inside the thick, high, outer wall surrounding the temple complex. Here, also, were the priests' houses, the magazines for storing the temple revenue, and a Sacred Lake where the priests could cleanse the god's utensils and perform their own ablutions before entering the temple.

In contrast to the decoration on the courtyard walls, which eulogized the king's prowess in battle and his relationship with the gods, the scenes on the walls of the innermost, sacred area of the temple show the king performing rites for the god. Frequently, these scenes were placed high on the walls and although finely executed were never intended as a decorative art form, their primary purpose was magical and ritual. They represented the different stages of each ritual activity for each area of the temple and when read in the correct sequence provide a clear summary of the rites found in each ritual. The very presence of the painted reliefs on the temple walls undoubtedly reassured the Egyptians of the continuation of these rituals, even if the actual performance of the rites was neglected or even abandoned, for their magical significance and potency was considered to be vitally important. The figures of the king and the deities in the reliefs were activated or 'brought to life' by means of a religious ceremony, in the same way as the statues in the tombs were 'revitalized' when the deceased was placed in his tomb. This ceremony was performed when the newly built temple was first handed over to its resident deity, and it was believed that all the wall-scenes, inscriptions and statues would then come to life. Even the inscriptions were thought to possess a certain magical force; by recharging the sacred environment of the temple they were believed to recreate the situation which had existed when the creation of the universe, the world and the first temple had taken place.

There were few changes in the design of the temple throughout the rest of Egypt's history. Even in the Ptolemaic and Roman periods when the Greeks and Romans ruled Egypt, the temples were constructed on the same basic plan as those of the New Kingdom. However, the later temples show best the use and purpose of the various sections of the building, for in most cases, the wall reliefs are better preserved and more informative and extensive than in the temples of Pharaonic Egypt. Both the mythology and the ritual use of the temple contributed to the Egyptians' conservatism in this respect and compelled them to reproduce as exactly as possible the forms found in the earliest temples.

Most of the architectural forms found in the Pharaonic and Ptolemaic temples relate to the mythology of the temple. This centred around the Egyptian concept of the universe and of creation. It is difficult to comprehend these ideas in the context of modern thought, because of one essential and important difference. Whereas we would accept the idea that society is forever changing and that each generation contributes new advances in learning and discovers fresh solutions to the problems of the day, the Egyptians regarded the universe and society as static concepts which worked according to set principles handed down to mankind at the beginning of time. Out of the chaos which had existed at the beginning, when darkness and water had prevailed, the world had been created; providing not only a physical refuge where men could live together, but also the pattern for a stable society. Concepts such as religion, law, ethics and the kingship were given to the Egyptians to enable them to regulate their lives, and the solutions to all the problems which they might encounter then or at some future date were made available on this 'First Occasion'. Future generations would simply have to recreate the conditions which were believed to have existed at this time, in order to obtain the answers to their problems. Change and development were therefore seen as unnecessary and even undesirable, for the ultimate aim of future generations was to restore perfectly the actual conditions of this primeval period. The temple, as a central feature of Egyptian religion, was thought to have been created at the beginning, and, as with the other concepts, there was no desire to change or to improve any aspect of its construction. Every Egyptian temple was regarded as a continuation and reflection of the first mythical temple where the first god had rested, and each stone temple attempted to recreate in detail the physical environment of the 'First Occasion'.

The temples built during the Graeco-Roman period contain inscriptions where these ideas are expressed. Lengthy texts, known as the 'Building Texts', occur in the temples at Edfu and at Denderah and these summarize the history of the temples, naming and describing the various halls and rooms and sometimes indicating their ritual use. The Edfu texts provide an account of the myth in which the creation of the temple is described. The portrait is of a time when darkness and swirling waters covered all the land; there were no gods and no life. Then, gradually, a low-lying mud island emerges from the waters and a piece of reed is washed ashore. Some demi-gods now make their appearance and salvage the reed, setting it in the ground near the water's edge. A falcon flies out of the darkness and settles on the reed; as the first god, his arrival on the island makes it a place of great sanctity, and the reed and its surrounding area become holy places which require protection. This is provided by the construction of a reed wall which encompasses the falcon on its reed perch. The island expands as the waters gradually recede, and additional rooms are attached to the original reed shelter. This finally becomes a complete reed temple, with rooms added at the front, sides and back. The floor in the shelter containing the god is at a slightly higher level than in the surrounding rooms, and this feature also appears in the stone temples where the reed sanctuary is represented by the shrine of the god, placed at the rear of the temple, and the level of the floor rises gradually from the halls at the front of the building to its highest level in the sanctuary area, and then falls away again in those chambers which are placed at the rear of the sanctuary.

The existing floor in many of the temples is not the original one and it is therefore impossible to determine the changes in the level. Nevertheless sufficient evidence survives to show that it was customary to construct the outer courts and the areas within the roofed section of the temple somewhat differently. In the temples of Luxor and Karnak, the whole of the enclosed temple, from the hypostyle halls to the rear of the temple, was built on a low platform. In other temples, the floor level was gradually raised from the hypostyle hall to the sanctuary, and then lowered again in the area to the rear of the sanctuary. This feature was achieved in various ways – sometimes a naturally sloping site was selected, or the halls and chambers approaching the sanctuary were floored with a series of pavements of gradually increased height. As one approached the sanctuary, the ceiling level was also lowered. A sense of awe was thus created as the worshipper approached the god's chamber. Both the pedestal-type of floor construction and the changing floor and ceiling levels were probably deliberate attempts to reproduce the primeval mound of the Island of Creation. Each 'new' temple was regarded as the original Island of Creation – a place of great magical potency – and so reflected the mythology in its structure.

Other mythological details also gave rise to architectural features in the temple and its surrounding complex. The waters which had surrounded the Island of Creation were recreated in the brick wall which enclosed the temple area. Built in sections it was decorated with wavy lines arranged in alternate concave and convex courses. Inside the temple, the ceiling, painted with stars, represented the sky above the island. If the decoration did not have either a specific ritual or formal purpose, it depicted the plant forms which would have flourished on the original island, for all art-forms within the temple, as in the tombs, were believed to be 'brought to life' by means of magic.

The columns, with their palmiform, lotiform or papyriform

capitals, would revert to the abundant vegetation of the Island of Creation. So criticism of the clumsiness and heaviness of their arrangement in close-packed clusters to support the roof of the hypostyle hall is entirely misplaced. Fewer, more elegant columns would have supported the roof equally well, but the main function of the columns was to symbolize the lush vegetation and fertility of the island landscape. Additional vitality was created by the plant forms shown in the reliefs at the base of some of the temple walls as though growing from the soil of the island represented by the temple floor.

The mythological explanation of the temple reflects, to some extent, the actual pattern of development from the reed shrines of the earliest periods to the magnificent stone temples of later times. Features found in the reed structures were retained as authentically as possible in the stone temples. The reed-columns, with palm-fronds, lotus and papyrus flowers attached at the top, were translated into the stone columns and their plant-form capitals. The reed supports had been set into hollowed-out stones or earthern sockets, and the shaft of the stone column was similarly placed on a separate stone base. The torus-roll seen in the stone architecture was derived from the bundles of reeds or palm sticks lashed into place to strengthen the corners of the lattice and mud walls of the early shrine. The tops of the palm-fronds had gently bent over, and this was repeated in the cavetto cornice found in the stone temples.

Apart from this explanation and its obvious historical associations, a secondary meaning was applied to the purpose of the Egyptian temple. It was probably derived from the mythological version, for the original Island of Creation had provided a place of rest and protection for the first deity. It was not difficult to encourage from this the idea that every temple was the house of its resident deity. The gods and goddesses took different forms but all temples shared a common role: each was a place of sanctity and rest for the resident deity, where the god's cult-statue could receive attention from his priests and where the divinity could be approached by man, through the person of the king.

The dead and the gods shared certain basic needs which the living were obliged to fulfil, and these needs were regarded as differing only in detail from those of the living. The dead and the gods possessed 'houses' – either tombs called 'Mansions of the Ka', or temples, referred to as 'Mansions of the gods'. The houses of the living, even the royal palaces, were constructed of mud-brick and wood, whereas, from an early date, stone was used for the construction of tombs and temples, since both were intended to last for eternity. The gods and the dead required food and drink, washing, time for rest and for recreation. This was provided for the dead by the ka-priests under the funerary cult; the divine cult served the same purpose for the gods and the rituals were performed in the temples by the priests who were called 'god's servants'.

It is therefore possible to see the same basic square plan in houses, tombs and temples, although the temple was modified by elongating the building to produce a central processional route for the rituals. Nevertheless each type of building contained private living quarters for the occupant, rooms for the storage of possessions and a reception area. The main door in the temple was usually situated on the main axis and through this, the ritual processions entered the building; side-doors enabled the priests to bring in the food and drink offerings. The procession passed through the hypostyle halls and the high priest would then approach the sanctuary, centrally situated at the rear of the temple, where the god's statue rested; here, he would perform the most important stages of the divine ritual.

The rituals which once took place inside these temples are still preserved in the scenes on the walls. The registers of scenes show rites performed in the main rituals and the accompanying inscriptions record the titles of the rites and the speeches of the deity and of the king. Read in the correct sequence, the scenes supply an abbreviated version of the rituals.

Generally there were two kinds of temple ritual. The first was performed daily and followed the same form and sequence for all temple deities throughout Egypt. The Daily Temple Ritual was performed for the resident deity of each temple and became a regular means of worship. It dramatized the normal routine of the day – each morning the officiating priest would enter the sanctuary and remove the cult-statue from its wooden shrine where it had rested for the night. He would remove the clothing and make-up of the previous day and fumigate the statue with incense. Various kinds of natron (salt) were then offered which could be chewed to cleanse the mouth, together with fresh clothing and make-up. The god's insignia was presented and finally, the priest placed the morning meal before the deity and withdrew from the sanctuary. Meals were probably offered again at mid-day and in the evening, before the cult-statue was returned to the shrine for the night.

In the mortuary temples, where the cult was performed for the dead king and for the previous rulers of Egypt, a corresponding ritual took place, which is now known as the 'Ritual of the Royal Ancestors'. Here, the food which was removed intact from the altar of the resident deity, at the conclusion of the Daily Temple Ritual, was taken to another area of the temple. After a series of preliminary rites, the food was now offered to the previous kings of Egypt, to obtain their support for the reign of the ruling king. The food, still untouched, was finally removed from the temple building and divided amongst the priests as payment for their services.

The second kind of temple ritual was the festival held usually on an annual basis. Each temple had its own festivals, some of which were unique to that temple, and which celebrated social events in the life of the god, or special occasions in the mythology connected with the deity. These varied considerably, from the great Osirian festival at Abydos, commemorating the annual death and resurrection of the god, to the conjugal visits between Hathor whose temple was at Denderah and her consort, Horus, the lord of Edfu. These festivals were colourful and exciting spectacles, in which not only the local inhabitants participated, but also the often large numbers of pilgrims who travelled long distances to attend the most important festivals. Unlike the daily rituals, confined to the temples and experienced by only a small number of priests, the festivals were enjoyed by the ordinary people, and a portable statue of the god, carried by his bearers in a wooden barque, would be paraded outside the temple and sometimes transported to the temple of a neighbouring deity.

Our knowledge of these rituals is largely based on the information found in the wall scenes, but even here, extreme care is needed in interpretation. The paintings show an idealized situation, in which the king performs every ritual in every temple throughout Egypt by himself, with no assistance from the priests, and certainly with no suggestion of delegating his duties to the high-priest. The role which the king played in temple ritual was undoubtedly of the utmost importance. In earliest times, the tribal ruler of each area would have attended to the needs of the tribal deity in its reed shrine, but as Egypt became an increasingly complex and united land, and one ruler became supreme, it was no longer possible for one man alone to fulfil all the state duties and religious commitments. The king may have performed the divine ritual once a day at the temple of the chief state god, in the capital city, although even this is doubtful, and he was probably present at the foundation ceremony of each new temple, but the performance of the regular rituals would have been delegated to the high-priest of the temple.

Nevertheless the myth continued that the king alone was the high-priest of every god. It was indeed essential that such a myth remained, because the king's participation in the temple ritual was one of its main principles. The king was unique in Egypt not because he or his predecessors had been sufficiently powerful to lead the country, but because he was Horus incarnate, the son of Re, and the divine heir. The gods had made him their son and ruler of Egypt so that he could carry out their wishes, and his half-divine nature made him the only man who could perform the rituals for the gods. In theory, he built every temple as a monument to its god; he acted as mediator between the gods and mankind; when he performed the Daily Temple Ritual, he personified Egypt and represented every Egyptian.

The relationship which was believed to exist between the gods and the Egyptians was essentially one of barter. Through the agency of the king, the Egyptians made food offerings, built temples and presented booty brought back from foreign campaigns. In return, the king hoped to receive the benefits of prosperity and power, eternal life and everlasting fame, and a safe and prosperous land with abundant harvests for his subjects. The king was regarded as the last of the gods but the first of men, who, by his divine nature, could act as the sole representative of mankind in the company of the gods. He could never abdicate, but he was never entirely divine; in all efficacious offerings and in the divine and mortuary cults, he acted as an intermediary.

The temple ritual was so important to the safety and well-being of Egypt that, not surprisingly, the men who really acted as the intermediaries in the rituals were themselves members of one of the most revered and influential sections of society. The priests were a powerful and hereditary group; their influence was underlined by the social, administrative and economic role which the temple played in society. It was at the same time both the hub of the community and yet segregated from the ordinary people. Each temple owned a considerable amount of land and sometimes vast estates and revenues. The top personnel of some of the most powerful temples, such as that of Amun at Karnak, became major political forces in the land, although, in theory, the temples were national institutions, governed by the king.

The king was required, as part of his religious obligation, to divert wealth to the temples, and this he did, partly by donating booty from his military expeditions, especially during the New Kingdom. Additional temple revenue came from dues from the provinces and from the southern gold mines. The dues were paid in grain, oil, wine, beer, metals and other materials; these were housed in extensive storehouses in the vicinity of the temple, and were recorded and administered by temple personnel. The economic power of the temples was further safeguarded by royal decrees allowing them certain exemptions and privileges.

Although the temple had a powerful influence on the society, it was never a religious community centre. Each town of any size had its own temple, dedicated to the local deity or group of gods. Large temples in the capital city and elsewhere were built to house the great state gods, but the ordinary people had little direct contact with the temple deities, and never attended regular services of worship. The temples were impressive architectural centrepieces to many of the towns, and may have provided the people with a place to visit occasionally, where they could pray to the god in the open forecourt of the temple or watch the colourful activities of the great festivals. The people may have perceived that the rituals which went on inside the temples safeguarded the very existence of Egypt, but the devotions of the ordinary man were most often addressed to humbler deities who had no temples nor divine cults. We call these minor deities 'household gods', since most homes would have contained a small shrine in their honour. The most famous were the dwarf-god, Bes, the god of love, marriage, dancing and jollification, and the hippopotamus-goddess, Tauert, responsible for fertility and childbirth. Unlike the temple deities, these grotesque figures were regarded as approachable, and they enjoyed considerable popularity and influence at all levels of society. The temple therefore had little direct contact with the people. The priests were primarily responsible for ministering to the needs of the temple deity and having no pastoral role in the community, were not required to offer instruction or guidance to those outside the temple precinct.

The temples nevertheless served a purpose as one of the great employers. Apart from the priests, singers and dancers were required, who may have accompanied some of the religious rites in a minor capacity; bakers, brewers, butchers and cooks were needed to prepare the food offerings; there was agricultural and textile work on the temple estates; craftsmen were needed to maintain the statues, reliefs and possessions of the god, and servants to clean the temple buildings. The size of the workforce varied according to the importance of the temple; that of Amun at Karnak employed a very large staff and administration to run the vast complex and its estates.

The priesthood included men who performed the rituals, who understood the liturgy, and who studied and taught their specialized subjects at the temples. It was usually a secondary profession, held on a hereditary basis by members of certain families. These men might be lawyers, doctors or scribes, and they would hold priesthoods related to their original profession. Lawyers often held the priesthood of Ma'at, goddess of justice and truth, and some doctors were priests of Sekhmet, a goddess closely associated with medicine. In addition to their other duties, they would enter the temple each year as temporary personnel. They were divided into four groups, each of which worked continuously for one month at the temple; in one year, each man would thus have completed three months of duty. For the remainder of the year, they would continue their main occupations outside the temple. They could marry and lead normal lives; taboos were only applied when they were resident in the temple. Then, the priest and his clothing had to be ritually 'pure', since he would come into direct contact with the god's house and personal belongings. The priests had specific skills to contribute, and subjects such as the liturgy, astronomy, astrology and the interpretation of dreams, geography, history, geometry and animal cults were studied in the temples. However, the most important contribution which the temple made to the secular community may well have been through its medical and educational role. It probably acted as a higher centre of learning to which students were sent to train as doctors, artists, scribes and lawyers. The temples possessed fine libraries which housed papyri covering many branches of learning and in general, they acted as storehouses of knowledge.

Some temples played an interesting role as centres of refuge where people could come in search of a miraculous cure. Sanatoria

were attached to some temples where petitioners were accommodated during their search for renewed health. They prayed to the
god, consulted the oracle to find answers to their problems, and
underwent a form of therapy which seems to have sometimes
brought relief.

The cultus and mortuary temples were thus primarily for ritual
purposes but they also played an important educational and social
role and appear to have been an essential part of Egyptian society.
They were places of spiritual potency where man could approach
the gods, and each was regarded as the recreation of the mythical
primordial island, and as the house of the resident deity. It was
only much later that the cosmological interpretation of the temple
developed, when it came to be regarded as a microcosm of the
universe, which deterred enemies and prevented evil from entering the sacred inner areas. Then the temple was compared to the
sky, with four corners and four quarters, the rooms to the left of
the building being sacred to the god's activities in the eastern parts
of the sky, the rooms to the right to his activities in the western
half of the sky. The pylons represented a great coffin in which the
sun slept, died and was re-born every day.

However, these were later embellishments, and the primary
function of these temples originated from the earliest reed shrines
and their associated offering rites. The sun-cult influenced all religious activities in Egypt to some extent including the daily temple
liturgy, but the sun-temples which flourished so briefly during the
Fifth dynasty must be regarded as a separate entity.

Although inscriptions indicate that at least six of these temples
were built during the Fifth dynasty, only the two examples built
by Userkaf and Niuserre have so far been discovered and excavated. Both are situated at Abu Gurob, but the temple of Niuserre
is better preserved since it was entirely stone-built, whereas Userkaf was constructed of limestone, limestone chips and mud.
Nevertheless they follow the same basic plan and probably owe
their origins to the important sun-temple dedicated to Re-Atum
which was built at Heliopolis, the centre of the sun-cult.

The temples were built at the edge of the desert; the summit of a
low mound providing a natural incline to meet the requirements
of the complex. At the lower level, a pavilion stood inside a large
enclosure and from this a covered causeway led gradually
upwards to a small chapel from which, on either side, covered
corridors extended to a wide, rectangular paved courtyard which

was open to the sky. Here, on a raised terrace, there was a low altar built of five large blocks of alabaster on which sacrifices were offered to the sun-god. The blood from the animals ran through channels cut in the pavement into nine alabaster basins. Immediately behind the altar stood the main feature of the complex and the object of the devotions carried out in the temple. This was a large, squat obelisk which differed in size and outline from the more famous obelisks of the New Kingdom cultus temples, whose slender forms grace several of the capital cities of the world today. The obelisks in the sun-temples were probably erected as copies of the famous, very ancient 'Benben' stone in the original sun-temple at Heliopolis. It has been suggested that obelisk meant 'the radiant one', and that it symbolized a sun-ray descending from the sky. In the temples of the Fifth dynasty, the obelisk was the cult-symbol of the sun-god where the power of the divinity could be confined and approached, as with the cult-statues in the later cultus temples. At this stage the obelisk appears to replace the pyramid as the emblem of Re, although probably the pyramid and the obelisk are variations of the original 'Benben'.

However, it is uncertain whether or not the obelisk was originally included in the sun-temples. It stood on a rectangular limestone podium, and this may itself have had a special significance when the first of these temples was built. One of the most important historical documents for the study of Egypt is the Palermo Stone (smaller fragments of which are stored in Cairo museum). It provides some information dating back to this period, and in his book, *The Pyramids of Egypt*, Dr I. E. S. Edwards states –

According to the Palermo Stone, a fragment of an inscription which recorded the official annals of the early kings of Egypt, Userkaf, one of the last kings named on the stone, built his sun-temple either in the fifth or in the sixth year of his short reign of seven years. The hieroglyphic sign which represents the temple, both in the entry on the Palermo Stone and in some other inscriptions dating from the beginning of the Fifth dynasty, seems to show only a podium without an obelisk, whereas inscriptions of the time of Neferirkare and of later times show both these features. In every probability therefore the obelisk was a later addition, and the suggestion has been made that the Mastaba-like construction which eventually served as its podium was intended by Userkaf to symbolize the primeval hill. Discoveries made in the course of excavation seem to support the evidence of the inscriptions, at least to the extent of indicating that the original plan of the enclosure was altered three times and also that the later designs included an obelisk, built of blocks of granite, which stood on a podium of limestone faced with ashlars of quartzite.

Outside the obelisk court in the temple of Niuserre, a brick boat-pit was discovered; this had once contained a solar barque probably intended for use by the sun-god when crossing the sky, and it has parallels in the boat-pits associated with the pyramids and with some of the earlier tombs. No such pit was found in the vicinity of Userkaf's temple.

From the architecture, it is difficult to assess the exact meaning and purpose of the complex. Although these temples were built some distance away from the pyramids constructed for the Fifth dynasty kings, the general layout and design of the sun-temples has been compared with that of the traditional pyramid complex. They both incorporate entrance buildings, covered causeways, solar boat burials, and solar emblems – here, in the sun-temple, the obelisk on its podium replaces the pyramid. The mortuary temple in the pyramid complex is replaced by the obelisk court with its sacrificial altar. One was a place of burial for the king and the other was a place of worship for the god, but they are similar in certain respects.

Again, the question of the origin of the sun-temples remains unanswered. They appear to have little in common with the earlier reed shrines or the consequent cultus temples so they may have an entirely separate origin. However, if the earliest sun-temple of Userkaf was originally constructed without an obelisk but with a podium representing the primeval Island of Creation, then there may be close links between these temples and the later cultus and mortuary temples. It can only be said that the solar temples were built and briefly flourished when the sun-cult reached its zenith; their main purpose was probably to provide places of worship for the god, based on the original solar shrine at Heliopolis. They would have required a smaller workforce for their construction than the pyramids which continued to be built during this period, albeit in an inferior manner with low-grade materials.

We know very little about the rituals performed in the sun-temples. The procession would have approached the sacred area through a covered causeway, but the climax of the ritual was carried out in the courtyard open to the sun-god. This differed from the rituals in the reed shrines or the later temples which were performed in dark, roofed areas. The obelisk replaced the cult-statue as the god's emblem, and sacrifices were offered on the altar below the podium, with the obelisk acting as a divine symbol to which the ritual could be directed. The ritual probably resembled the other funerary and divine rituals, in which food offerings were presented to the dead or to the god. The Palermo Stone relates that King Userkaf daily sacrificed two oxen and two geese on the altar of the sun-temple. The slaughtering of the animals and birds was carried out in a separate enclosure to the north of the altar where there was a series of magazines for the storage of other offerings.

If the main use of these temples centred around the ritual worship of the sun, other possible uses of the buildings are suggested by the wall reliefs. Some of the finest examples of Old Kingdom art have been discovered in the carved and painted wall reliefs of the temple of Niuserre at Abu Gurob, although no examples were found in Userkaf's neighbouring complex. The reliefs from Niuserre's temple, now kept in the museums of Cairo and Berlin, were discovered in three areas of the temple – in the covered corridor of the causeway, in the extension which occupied the east and south sides of the obelisk court, and in the chapel at the end of the corridor. The quality of the reliefs was superb, giving an opportunity to assess the standard of craftsmanship achieved during this period, but the content was of equal importance and interest. This included the ceremonial connected with the foundation of the temple and the king's jubilee festival, for which a more complete scenario occurs here than in any other building of this period. The seasons are also shown, represented as people bringing offerings to the sun-god or the king, and they are accompanied by minor deities or personifications of the districts of Egypt. These reliefs depict the many and varied deities who formed the pantheon at this time as well as the flora and fauna created by the sun-god.

In addition to its use as a place for regular worship of the sun-god, the content of these scenes suggests that the temple was regarded as a building where the king could celebrate his jubilee festivals after death.

The sun-temples of the Fifth dynasty were apparently unique to that period, closely linked with the powerful solar cult. They do not seem to have been imitated in later dynasties, but when a solar cult again thrived towards the end of the Eighteenth dynasty, new temples were built which differed from the traditional cultus and mortuary temples; it will be interesting to consider what influence, if any, the Old Kingdom temples exerted over these later buildings.

# 5  Myth, Magic and Ritual

Architectural and archaeological remains provide information about the sun-cult, but literary sources also contain many references to the role played by Re in both ritual and mythology.

One of the most interesting legends found in Egyptian literature recounts the events which are supposed to have occurred immediately before the rise of the solar cult in the Fifth dynasty. This tale is found in the Westcar Papyrus which probably dates from the Second Intermediate period, long after the events which it describes had taken place. The elements of the story must have been handed down from generation to generation and we can imagine that it was often recited to rapt audiences during the Old Kingdom by public story-tellers.

The story is set in the time of the Old Kingdom, and it recalls the wonderful deeds performed by the magicians of the past. King Cheops, the Fourth dynasty builder of the Great Pyramid, asks each of his sons to relate a magical incident to him at his Court. Prince Chephren (who later became the king who built the second pyramid at Gizeh) is first to tell his story. It concerns the chief magician Ubaoner who lived in the time of King Nebka, a predecessor of Cheops, and how he uses his magical skills to catch and kill his wife's lover. Then Prince Baufre recalls one of the deeds of Zazamonkh who was chief magician in the reign of Sneferu, Cheops' immediate predecessor. The king had taken some fair maidens sailing on the palace lake; one of the girls loses a fish-pendant of malachite which falls from her neck into the water. She is dismayed at her loss, and the magician is called in. He proceeds to fold up the water of the lake and reclaim the pendant from the bottom of the lake before restoring the waters to their rightful position.

Prince Hardedef then steps forward; he is known from other sources to have been a famous sage of the Old Kingdom. He begins – 'Hitherto hast thou heard only examples of what they knew that have gone before (us), and one knoweth not the truth from falsehood. But even in thine own time, there is a magician.'

The king then asks Hardedef to bring this man to the palace. The prince journeys by river to the home of the magician, Dedi, reputed to be of considerable age. Prince Hardedef persuades the old man to accompany him to the Royal Residence, where, in the grand pillared hall, the king awaits them in eager anticipation. 'Is it true, what is said, that thou canst put on again a head that hath been cut off?' asks the king. A goose is brought in and its head is cut off; its body and its head are placed on opposite sides of the hall, and 'Dedi said his say of magic. Thereupon the goose stood up and waddled, and its head likewise.' Dedi then successfully demonstrates his magical skills by performing the same feat with a duck and an ox.

This entertaining narrative now leads up to the main point of the story which appears to be the justification of the claim to rule Egypt by the kings of the Fifth dynasty, who succeeded Cheops' own family. The magician is reputed to know the number of the locks of the sanctuary of Thoth, which, as god of wisdom, Thoth had originally invented to make his sanctuary secure. Cheops wishes to safeguard his own pyramid, and he asks Dedi for this information, but the magician says he does not know the numbers. However, he tells the king that they are kept in a chest of flint in Heliopolis, and although he will be unable to bring them to Cheops, he will send another – 'It is the eldest of the three children who are in the belly of Red–dedet that will bring it thee.'

The story then continues –

And his majesty said: 'But I desire that thou say who she is, this Red–dedet.' And Dedi said: 'It is the wife of a priest of Re of Sakhebu, that hath conceived three children of Re, lord of Sakhebu. He hath told her that they will exercise this excellent office in this entire land, and that the eldest of them will be high-priest in Heliopolis.' Then his majesty's heart grew sad thereat. And Dedi said: 'Pray, what is this mood, O King, my lord? Is it because of the three children? Then I say unto thee: thy son, his son, and then one of them.'

In this way, the story asserts the divine origin of the kings of the Fifth dynasty; the first three kings of this dynasty are acclaimed as the offspring of the god Re whom he has begotten to rule Egypt in preference to Cheops' descendants. It is not surprising that Cheops is dismayed, although Dedi's prophecy assures him that his own son Chephren will succeed him, and his grandson Mycerinus will follow, before the new line of kings is instated. The story is historically inaccurate in that two other kings ruled between the death of Mycerinus and the first king of the Fifth dynasty, but as a simple tale it would be sufficiently realistic to impress the listeners of later generations who had probably only heard tell of the three great pyramid-builders of the Fourth dynasty. The propaganda which the author of the story wishes to put across – that the origin of the Fifth dynasty was divine and that the state cult of the Heliopolitan sun-god was supreme – is cleverly concealed here in an entertaining and lively tale which would undoubtedly have captured the interest of its popular audience. This and other examples, show the Egyptians were skilful at ensuring support for the king of the period and the legitimacy of his right to rule was disseminated at all levels of society.

The story now continues with Cheops' plan to visit the temple of Re at Sakhebu – a town in the vicinity of Memphis and Heliopolis; perhaps his intention was to prevent the prophecy from coming true, although no further details are given. Dedi helps the king to make the journey there, and Cheops instructs Prince Hardedef to reward the magician by making him a member of his household and ensuring that henceforth the old man receives an ample allowance.

The final part of the tale describes the delivery of Red-dedet and the birth of her divine triplets. Re sends deities to assist at the birth – these are Isis, Nephthys, Mesekhent (the goddess of birth), Heket (a frog-goddess), and Khnum, who fashioned mankind and the gods on his potter's wheel. They are ushered into the house by Rewoser, husband of Red-dedet, and are shown into the birth chamber. The goddesses hasten the birth of the first child; Isis says '"Be not hasty in her womb, as truly as thou art named User-ref." This child slipped forth on to her hands, a child of one cubit with strong bones; the royal titulary of his limbs was of gold, and his head-cloth of true lapis-lazuli. They washed him, cut his navel-string, and laid him upon a sheet upon a brick. And Mesekhent drew near to him and she said: "A king that will exercise the kingship in the entire land." And Khnum gave health to his body.'

The births of the other two children are also described, and their names pronounced by Isis as 'Sah-re' and 'Keku'. It is obviously intended that the triplets mentioned in this story should be identified with the first three rulers of the Fifth dynasty – Userkaf, Sahure and Kakai (Neferirkare); the children are born wearing the royal headcloth, and the titulary with was usually assumed on reaching the throne is already present on their limbs, inlaid in gold.

Before finally leaving the children, the goddesses fashion three royal crowns for them, which they place in the barley and hide in a locked chamber.

The manuscript ends with an account of the betrayal which Red-dedet's handmaiden plans. The girl is sent to the locked chamber to fetch some barley, where she hears 'the sound of singing, music, dancing, rejoicing and all that is done in a king's honour.' She reports this to Red-dedet who goes into the chamber in search of the cause of the noise; she discovers that the festivities are taking place inside the corn-bin, and she locks the bin and hides it inside a closet. A few days later, the handmaiden incurs her mistress's displeasure and receives a beating. The girl now wishes to obtain revenge, and she tells the other servants – '. . . she has born three kings. I will go and tell it unto the Majesty of King Cheops'.

She attempts to involve her brother in this betrayal, but he also beats her. When the girl leaves him, she goes down to the river to draw some water and is seized by a crocodile. Her brother tells Red-dedet of his sister's fate, and here the manuscript breaks off and the end of the story is lost.

The story is written in popular language and was undoubtedly very successful amongst the ordinary people. It presents a most favourable account of the kings of the Fifth dynasty – not only is it prophesied that Cheops' line will be terminated; it indicates that any attempt by Cheops to prevent this will be unsuccessful. Also, the kings of the Fifth dynasty are portrayed as religious rulers whom the god has begotten, whereas the kings of the Fourth dynasty, especially Cheops, have been represented as tyrants in later legends. Before the birth of the divine triplets, Re tells the goddesses of the good deeds which these kings will perform – 'Up, go ye and deliver Red-dedet of the three children that are in her womb that will exercise this excellent office in this entire land. They will build your temples, they will replenish your libation-tables, and they will make great your offerings.'

We have already seen that the tale is not historically accurate and that only the most important kings of the Fourth dynasty are mentioned. Again, there is no historical evidence to support the story's claim that the mother of the first three kings of the Fifth dynasty was the wife of a simple priest of Re, and other evidence shows that Userkaf was the father of Sahure and Neferirkare although they are here described as divine triplets. Nevertheless the story is successful in conveying the information that the power of the Heliopolitan sun-cult was growing rapidly, that the sun-god had created the rulers of the Fifth dynasty, and (a fact which is borne out by other evidence) that these rulers venerated Re and built new temples for him.

Re's rise to power during the Fifth dynasty had its foundation in events which occurred during the Old Kingdom. This was the establishment of sacred colleges which grew up around the cults of various important deities. The wall scenes in the private tombs of the Old Kingdom show everyday activities which the deceased noble hoped would continue for him in the afterlife, but the deities were not represented. However, many deities are shown in the royal temple reliefs of the Fifth dynasty, and the traditional appearance and forms of the gods seem already to have been established. Some deities are fully humanized; others retain some aspects of their ancient animal forms; and others are recognizable by their symbols. The worship of deities continued on a local basis and many different gods and goddesses existed side by side and were linked in a loose association. The royal sun-cult flourished and the popular appeal and vivid mythology of the god Osiris undoubtedly increased his impact on the Egyptians. Although these two gods could be seen as rivals during this period, there is no clear evidence of political or military confrontation between the supporters of the two cults during the Old Kingdom. Other deities also achieved the status of 'State-gods', but no one divinity was sufficiently influential amongst all classes to become their chief god or to possess a temple in every town or locality.

Some attempt was now made to rationalize this loose association of deities. The priests at the sacred colleges in the most influential cult centres tried to form groups of gods who would act as subordinates and assistants in the mythologies woven around the principal gods of the centres. The most famous of these groups were the Great and Little *enneads* of Heliopolis and the *ogdoad* of Hermopolis. The central theme of the myths was the creation of the universe, and each priesthood invented a cosmogony in which they tried to maintain the supremacy of their own cult-centre and its principal god. The god became the creator-god of the universe who had triumphed over the state of emptiness and chaos which had prevailed. The other deities associated with his mythology became direct descendants of the principal god, each with his own role in the establishment of order. On the First Occasion, mankind was given the ingredients of law, justice, ethics and religion to create a good, stable society, in addition to the physical environment where they could live. After creation had taken place, the gods ruled on earth, before handing over their rule to the king who was the divine heir and successor. He was required to uphold justice and to rule Egypt according to the principles of Ma'at, the goddess who personified truth, justice and righteousness and the correct order and balance in all things. She ensured that the conditions which had prevailed when the earth was ruled by the gods would continue; all the people and even the king were subject to her principles. The Egyptian concept of a healthy society rested upon the right balance being retained in all aspects of life and nature.

Three important cosmogonies developed during the Old Kingdom stimulated by the priesthoods of Heliopolis, Memphis and Hermopolis and centred around the principal gods of these towns. The Theban cosmogony was introduced during the New Kingdom, when the great temple of Amen-Re at Karnak reached its zenith and the cult of Amen-Re became supreme. Here, however, we shall confine ourselves to the Old Kingdom cosmogonies.

The best known system was that of Heliopolis, developed by the priests of Re. In this cosmogony, the association of cosmic and other deities is clearly demonstrated. There were two groups of nine gods – the Greater *ennead*, which consisted of Re-Atum, Shu and Tefnut, Geb and Nut, Osiris, Isis, Nephthys, and Seth and the Little *ennead* which included lesser deities under the direction of Horus. Re, the sun-god, had taken over the cult centre of On or Iwnw (Heliopolis). He assumed the attributes of an earlier deity – Atum – with whom he had become completely identified by the time the Pyramid Texts were inscribed in the pyramids of the later Old Kingdom.

The Pyramid Texts are the main source for the Heliopolitan doctrine, but their primary purpose was to ensure, by magical means, the safe passage of the king to the next world. The texts assume prior knowledge of the doctrine and illustrate that the nature deities – sky, earth, wind, sun, moon and stars – played important roles in this cosmogony, while other, non-cosmic deities had minor parts. The details are often inconsistent and the information relating to the geneaology is sometimes contradictory. Nevertheless we can outline the basis of the Heliopolitan cosmogony.

Atum, first god of Heliopolis, emerged from Nun, the great primordial ocean; he is either said to be the child of Nun, or to be self-created, brought forth by his own act of will. His first concern was to create a hill or mound on which he could stand, and the Heliopolitan priests claimed that their temple stood on the mound which the deity had formed. Since he was associated with Re, Atum also brought light to the state of darkness and chaos. Taking the form of the mythological Bennu bird, the god then alighted on the Benben – the squat obelisk which became the symbol of the sun-god at Heliopolis and which was regarded as a central, sacred feature of the cult.

Re-Atum began the process of creation by begetting his own children; he was regarded as bi-sexual, having both male and female characteristics, and by masturbation he was able to create Shu, the god of air, whom he spat out, and Tefnut, goddess of moisture, whom he vomited out. They were born either on the primeval hill or in the waters of the ocean and in turn became the parents of Geb, the earth god, and Nut, the sky-goddess. These first five deities of the *ennead* personified the main forces of nature and they were all cosmic deities. However, the last four – the children of Geb and Nut – had human rather than cosmic associations. We meet them elsewhere, as the main characters in the Osiris myth – Osiris, Isis, Nephthys and Seth. Osiris and Isis become the parents of Horus. Their presence in the Heliopolitan cosmogony could be an attempt by the priests of Re to include them in the doctrines as subordinates to Re-Atum, whose power and supremacy Osiris was soon to rival.

A more immediate threat to Heliopolis was posed by the theological centre at Memphis. The priests here tried to prove that a sequence of events involving their principal god, Ptah, preceded the Heliopolitan doctrine. It identified Ptah as the Father who was also Nun. He begot a daughter, Naunet, by whom he fathered his son, Atum – the creator-god of Heliopolis. Atum then created Shu and Tefnut, but his role was secondary to that of Ptah who was creator of the world and the 'heart' and 'tongue' of the Heliopolitan *ennead*. His thought and will were expressed through his heart and his command through his tongue, and thus he created the universe. Atum was merely his agent, and was sometimes replaced in this role by Horus and Thoth. Ptah was regarded as the sole creator of the world, and of the gods, their cult-centres and their images. He also made the nomes and the cities, and all physical requisites such as food and drink. He was the 'Lord of Truth' who created divine utterance and established a code of ethics. Ptah became closely associated with Osiris at Memphis and with other funerary gods, but his priesthood failed to elevate his cult to an unrivalled supremacy, probably because the mythology was too intellectual for ordinary people to identify with him.

The third great centre was Hermopolis; here, a variety of creation myths developed which were nevertheless compatible. The Hermopolitan cosmogony also claimed it was the system from which the others had derived. The central feature was the *ogdoad* – a group of eight deities – who included four male gods usually depicted with frogs' heads, and their female counterparts who were serpent-headed. The gods were Nun (the primordial ocean), Huh (eternity), Kuk (darkness) and Amun (air, or that which is hidden). The goddesses were Naunet, Hauhet, Kauket and Amaunet. These eight deities created the world and then ruled over it during the period immediately after the First Occasion. They finally passed into the underworld where their actions in causing the Nile to flow and the sun to rise ensured the continuation of life on earth. Another version stated that the universe had originated inside the Cosmic Egg – this had been laid on the primeval mound either by a goose or by an ibis which was a form of Thoth, the great god of Hermopolis. Re, the sun-god, emerged from the egg in the form of a bird, or, alternatively the egg was filled with air. Yet another myth claimed that life had started from a lotus flower, which the *ogdoad* had created. The flower rose out of the 'Sea of Knives' – the temple lake at Hermopolis. Inside the petals was the child Re who became creator of the world, or a scarab-beetle which changed into a boy and whose tears became mankind.

Other creation myths featured goddesses such as Isis and Hathor, or Khnum, the ram-headed god of Elephantine, who created men and women from clay and fashioned them on his potter's wheel. However, the cosmogonies of Heliopolis, Memphis and Hermopolis remained the most important, and, although each stressed the importance of its own cult-centre and priesthood and the creative role of its principal god, they contained the same basic concepts. They all referred to Nun and the emergence of the primeval mound which was to become such an important feature in the mythology of the temple. Each priesthood claimed that its temple was built on the site of this first place of creation and was therefore a source of great spiritual potency. The Egyptians seem to have regarded creation as a gradual process rather than a single act, although the birth of the universe and life had occurred on a specific occasion. The process had brought into existence the earth and the heavens, the underworld, the gods, the king and mankind, and also abstract notions such as law, religion and ethics. The sun and the Nile were seen by the Egyptians as essential in producing the physical conditions of life they knew and all the important cosmogonies accepted the creative role of the sun-god.

The mythology associated with the sun-god is rich and varied. Even the origin of Re is interpreted in many different ways, but such inconsistency was quite acceptable to Egyptian thought. Identified with Atum, Re was believed to have created himself by his own will; he appeared as a Bennu bird at Heliopolis, and, according to the Hermopolitan doctrine, arrived in a lotus flower. He is also described as the son of Geb and Nut, being born as a cow, laid in an egg, or as the complete creation of Ptah. He became the father of Shu and Tefnut, of Hathor, of Osiris, Seth and Horus, and of Ma'at.

Some of the myths emphasize the part played by his sacred eye. Re's sweat and tears were supposed to have formed mankind and all creatures. The eye could act independently and on one occasion it disappeared alone, so Re sent out Shu and Tefnut to find the eye and return it to him; the eye however resisted their attempts at capture, and shed tears which became mankind. Another time, Shu and Tefnut being lost, Atum dispatched the eye to discover them; when they returned, he placed the eye on his forehead. Another account tells how the eye became a uraeus serpent; it was placed on the brow of Re, and was eventually worn on the forehead of every Egyptian king as a royal symbol. It was believed that the royal uraeus would spit venom and harm any man who sought to do evil to the king.

The life cycle of Re which so closely resembled the daily passage of the sun was a subject around which many myths grew. Re, as a young man, had ruled over the earth during the period when the gods had lived on earth. He was powerful and visited all parts of his realm every day. He fought and finally beheaded Apophis, a serpent who had assisted Re's enemies in their attempts to kill him. However, he became old and his rule was no longer strong and respected; other deities mocked at him and men planned his downfall. His eye then took the form of a goddess – either Hathor or Sekhmet, the lion-headed divinity – and set off to destroy his enemies. Despite victory, Re had become tired of life and he left the earth to return to the heavens; Thoth, the moon-god, ruled in his place. In the heavens, Re created an eternal world which the dead – at first the kings and then others – sought to enter after death. Re experienced re-birth daily, when he arose every morning from the mountains or from the ocean behind the mountains

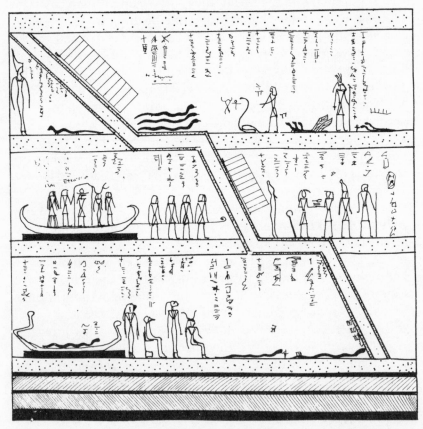

Figure 21 The 4th hour of the sun's voyage. Part of the Book of Am-Duat, used as mural decoration in the Tomb of Tuthmosis III in the Valley of the Kings. 18th dynasty

at the edge of the world. Accompanied by the gods who acted as crew-members, Re sailed across the heavens in his day-barque; he encountered his chief enemy, Apophis, and fought a battle which he always won. The course of his life on earth – progressing from a young, vigorous man to an aged and impotent ruler – was reflected in his daily development from birth at dawn, through maturity, to old age and death at nightfall. Each day, the sun rose by coming up from the underworld, and each night, it set by passing into the underworld. For the twelve hours of darkness, the sun-god was transported in his night-barque through the underworld, accompanied again by a crew of gods. Here, he confronted dangers more terrifying than those which he had met by day. His life was threatened by serpents and demons and he once again faced Apophis. At each hour, the goddess of the hour opened the gate for him to pass into the next province, and directed various deities and demons to tow the barque, for there was no wind in the underworld to move the boat. Once he had passed through the twelve divisions of the night, the god passed once again into the sky, and the solar disc – his symbol – was transferred to the day-barque.

Figure 22 Re's voyage in the Underworld. An unfinished wall scene in the tomb of Pharaoh Horemheb, in the Valley of the Kings. 18th dynasty

Other explanations of the daily solar cycle suggested that Re was the son of the sky-goddess, Nut, who took the form of a cow; and that Re was born as a calf every morning and swallowed up again by his mother every evening.

Re had various aspects; as a young man, personifying the sun at dawn, he was known as 'Khepri'. This name is derived from the hieroglyphic word *ḫpr*, which is the word used for the scarab-beetle and for the verb 'to come into existence.' Khepri is often shown as a scarab pushing the disc of the sun in front of him. The link between the verb 'to come into existence' and the sun-god in his renewed form is obvious; the connection with the scarab-beetle is less apparent. The Egyptians adopted the scarab-beetle as the symbol of regeneration because of an understandable but mistaken observation. The egg of the beetle is laid in the insect's own dung, so that when the new beetles appeared they seemed

Figure 23 Painting from the tomb of Sennedjem at Thebes, showing the falcon-headed god Re, adorned with the sun's disc and uraeus, and Harakhte, seated on a calf, who passes between the trees marking the horizon. 19th dynasty

self-generated. The Egyptians were further confused in believing that the new generation of beetles actually issued from the ball of food supply which the beetle pushed along in front of it.

Atum was another aspect of Re – he was the original deity worshipped at Heliopolis, and was also usually regarded as the setting sun. The god became 'Auf' (corpse) during his night journey in the underworld. The sun-god was usually represented as a solar disc, sometimes carried in the sacred barque, but he was also shown as a falcon-headed man. In this form he was identified with the sky-god Horus and became the deity Re-Harakhte. He usually wore the sun's disc on his head and the uraeus on his brow.

Perhaps the most important role of the sun-god was as the royal protector. He supported the right of the king to rule, maintained order and protected the king against his enemies. The kings of Egypt based their right to rule Egypt on two counts – they were incarnations of Horus, son of Osiris, and every king was the son and heir of Re.

Much of our knowledge of the early mythology is gained from the 'Pyramid Texts'. These were first introduced into the pyramid complex of king Unas, the last king of the Fifth dynasty, who was buried at Saqqara. They were hieroglyphic inscriptions, carved on the walls of the vestibule and parts of the burial chamber of Unas' pyramid. They were intended to secure a danger-free afterlife for the king and the queen. Similar texts occur in the Sixth dynasty pyramids of Teti, Pepy I, Merenre, Pepy II and those of his three queens, and the pyramid of King Ibi who probably reigned during the First Intermediate period.

The kings of the Fifth and Sixth dynasties had become fully aware of the dangers of providing for their continued existence after death. The grandeur and magnificence of earlier complexes had attracted the unwelcome attention of tomb robbers and no adequate protective devices had been found. The mortuary priests and their descendants all too frequently shirked their responsibility to provision the tombs of both kings and commoners. In the later part of the Old Kingdom, the kings may therefore have decided to resort to the use of magical formulae to protect themselves, and to have these texts inscribed on the inner walls of their pyramids. The spiritual and magical power of the texts was intended to guarantee the king his resurrection and re-birth into a solar eternity.

These texts form the oldest collection of written religious

material in the world. They contain fragments of myths and legends, historical references, astronomical lore, geography, cosmology, magic and morals, rituals and festivals. The compilation of various doctrines and beliefs from several different periods shows little apparent attempt to arrange the material in a logical order. This means that the statements, read as such, often contradict each other. However, another opinion maintains that the arrangement of the texts as a whole is systematic. The texts are seen to reflect a gradual process of development in the myths, beliefs and customs relating to the death, burial and resurrection of the king. Few spells are repeated in all the pyramids, although most occur more than once. The priests may have recited the spells as they passed by in procession, accompanying the king's body to the burial chamber on the day of burial. The texts were possibly arranged on the walls in a certain order and position, to be visible to the deceased, lying in his sarcophagus, and thus to assist him in his resurrection. There is no evidence that non-royal persons of this period ever had such texts in their tombs, although the Coffin Texts, which were used to decorate the coffins of commoners during the Middle Kingdom, were derived from them. Eventually, the content of the Pyramid Texts became even more widely available when, in the New Kingdom, the Theban *Book of the Dead* was drawn from these earlier concepts.

The king's divinity, the satisfactory completion of his burial and funerary ritual, and his successful ascent to heaven after death were central features of Egyptian religion. The Pyramid Texts were intended to ensure this ascent by means of magic; spells were included to provide various aids such as wings, steps or ramps. One such passage reads –

He that flieth flieth! He flieth away from you, ye men. He is no longer on earth, he is in the sky.

Another passage describes his ascent to heaven –

A ramp to the sky is built for him, that he may go up to the sky thereon. He goeth up on the smoke of the great exhalation. He flieth as a bird, and he settleth as a beetle on an empty seat that is in the ship of Re . . .

By asserting the king's own powers or by calling on the gods for assistance, the texts also attempted to guarantee the king's survival and immortality once he had reached the heavens. The king is now a god and in his new role is an equal who can seize heaven. As the texts relate –

The gods are afraid of him, for he is older than the Great One. He it is who hath power over his seat.

The texts then illustrate a dramatic solution to the power struggle between the king and the gods; in the so-called Cannibal Hymn, the king devours the gods in order to obtain their powers for himself –

He it is that eateth their magic and swalloweth their lordliness. Their great ones are for his morning meal, their middle-sized ones for his evening meal, and their little ones for his night meal. Their old men and their old women are assigned for his fumigation. The Great Ones who are in the north of the sky, they place for him the fire to the kettles, that which is under them being the thighs of their eldest ones. The sky-dwellers serve him, and the cooking pots are wiped out for him with the legs of their women.

In general, the formulae used in the texts are quite short but in some cases, spells are obviously combined and the content is often confused and even contradictory. The Pyramid Texts were written in archaic language and therefore some difficulty occurs in translating the meaning and allusions of some of the passages. However, they provide one of the most important and comprehensive sources for the study of early religious belief in Egypt. As in other Egyptian writings, older beliefs and ideas which had proved their worth were not discarded, but were combined with new thoughts wherever necessary, to increase the efficacy and magical potency of the whole. The texts were probably compiled by the Heliopolitan priests between the Third and Fifth dynasties. Heliopolitan and Osirian doctrines are incorporated with older beliefs which probably pre-dated the union of Upper and Lower Egypt and which perhaps began as oral traditions written down before they were included in the Pyramid Texts. Historical references in the texts provide some evidence that the spells were composed at different periods, with some of the earliest concerned with the hostilities which preceded the unification of Egypt. The cannibalistic references are believed to date from the Predynastic period and this is supported by a reference in the Cannibal Hymn which mentions the assembling of the bones of the dead. This must reflect a time and situation which existed before the first known attempts at mummification during the early dynasties.

However, the main concern of the texts is with the celestial afterlife of the king. We have already considered the possibility that solar and stellar cults merged and that the step pyramid (perhaps the symbol of a star cult) was incorporated within the later true pyramid which was closely associated with the solar cult. In the Pyramid Texts, there is an indication that a stellar and a solar cult may have merged together, probably at an early date, and their similarity as sky-cults may have encouraged this. The king is identified both with Re – 'He encompasseth the sky like Re' – and with the Great Ones who live in the sky as stars –

He is more glorified than the Glorified Ones, more excellent than the Excellent Ones, more enduring than the Enduring Ones.

Osirian concepts, which include an afterlife in the underworld, are also featured in the texts. Osiris, as ruler of the dead, is referred to as living in the sky, and the king is identified with Osiris as well as with Re –

Thou hast thine heart, Osiris; thou hast thy feet, Osiris; thou hast thine arm, Osiris. He hath his own heart; he hath his own feet; he hath his own arm. A ramp to the sky is built for him, that he may go up to the sky thereon.

The fact that Osiris is included in these Heliopolitan texts reflects the increased popularity and influence of this god towards the latter part of the Old Kingdom. But the apparent stability of both the state and the kingship does not indicate that any deep division existed between the cults of Re and Osiris at this time. However, it is possible that the sun god had become so powerful that the king considered it expedient to introduce Osirian elements into the official religion in an attempt to curb Re's omnipotence. Perhaps the king hoped to identify with Osiris as judge and god of the underworld – a position which Re, although supreme in heaven, could not threaten.

Some scholars interpret the different doctrines in the Pyramid Texts in terms of historical and political developments and of confrontations between rival religious groups, but the evidence available is scanty and confused. It may be wiser to regard this compilation as a typically Egyptian solution to the basic problem of ensuring the king's immortality – by including as many spells as possible to increase the magical potency and success of the texts.

Throughout history various hymns were addressed to Re, and

these reflect the progress of the god's cult. The earliest known example is preserved in the Pyramid Texts; it is a repetitive hymn in which the deity is addressed with the words 'Awake in peace!' which are followed each time by a different name or descriptive title. The chanting of the hymn must have been monotonous and was probably used to arouse the god in his temple each morning. Such hymns may have developed out of the chants with which the women awoke their village chieftain during the Predynastic period. In the Pyramid texts, the hymn occurs in this form –

> Awake in peace, thou Cleansed One, in peace!
> Awake in peace, thou Eastern Horus, in peace!
> Awake in peace, thou Eastern Soul, in peace!
> Awake in peace, Harakhti, in peace!
>
> Thou sleepest in the evening barque,
> Thou awakest in the morning barque,
> For thou art he that overlooketh the gods,
> There is no god that overlooketh thee!

Most other important hymns date from the New Kingdom, although their content is probably taken from older sources. By this period, it had become the custom to include two hymns in the tomb, either inscribed on one of the walls or written on papyrus, forming part of the *Book of the Dead*. One hymn was dedicated to the morning sun and the other to the evening sun; both were provided to enable the deceased to continue to enjoy the sun's presence. One of the hymns to the morning sun, taken from a version of the *Book of the Dead*, starts with greeting –

Adoration of Re, when he ariseth in the eastern horizon of heaven.

It tells how Re is praised by the *ennead* and by men –

Mankind rejoiceth at him, the Souls of Heliopolis shout joyfully to him; the Souls of Buto and Hieraconpolis extol him.

The 'Souls' are the deities of the ancient sun–cult centre and of the Predynastic capitals of Upper and Lower Egypt. The hymn continues with an expression of joy by the animals who welcome the sun's daily appearance –

The apes adore him; 'Praise to thee!' say all wild beasts with one consent.

The sun then overcomes his enemies, represented by the clouds, and the hymn ends with the words –

Give me light, that I may see thy beauty.

The evening hymn starts with a similar address –

Adoration of Re-Harakhti, when he setteth in the western horizon of heaven. Praise to thee, O Re, when thou settest, Atum, Harakhti!

The hymn describes how the evening barque and its crew are joyful and how the enemies of the sun have been overcome. The sun sets in the 'horizon of Manun' which was a legendary mountain situated in the west. The god then passes into the underworld, where the dead rejoice because his presence drives away their afflictions. They show their gratitude by towing the god's ship through the underworld – a necessity because in the dark and oppressive provinces of the underworld, there is not a breath of wind to hasten the journey.

Perhaps the most impressive hymn to Re is one which is actually addressed in part to another god – Amun. The Great Hymn to Amun is written on a papyrus which dates from the reign of Amenophis II of the Eighteenth dynasty. In order to give their god unrivalled power, the Theban princes who became kings of Egypt and founders of the Eighteenth dynasty associated their own local god, Amun, with the sun-god Re, thus creating the supreme deity Amen-Re. This god assumed far more of the characteristics of the sun-god than those of Amun and this is apparent in the hymn, where the sun-god is hailed by all his old names –

Praise to thee, O Re, Lord of Truth. Thou whose chapel is hidden, Lord of gods. Khepre in his barque, who gave command and the gods came into being. Atum, who created mankind. . .

He also fulfils the same functions as Re; he sails over the celestial ocean –

Lord of the ship of evening and of the ship of morning; they traverse Nun for thee in peace.

and the fight with Apophis continues –

That dragon, an end is made of his going. The gods shout for joy, and the crew of Re is content.

The hymn resembles the older hymns to Re in both style and content – the god is addressed and praised in his many forms and the Great Hymn is probably an amalgamation of these earlier compositions, with little attempt to organize the material.

New elements in this hymn, however, place a different emphasis on the god's abilities and powers. These also occur in other literary sources of the New Kingdom and stress the creative role of the god –

Thou art the Sole One, who made all that is, the One and Only who made what existeth. Men issued forth from his two eyes, and from his mouth, the gods came into being.

He who made herbage for the cattle and the fruit-tree for men. He who made that whereon live the fish in the river and the birds which (inhabit) the firmament.

He who giveth breath to him that is in the egg, and sustaineth the son of the worm . . .

The gods make obeisance under thy majesty, and extol the might of their creator.

Another new aspect is his loving and caring nature –

He who heareth the prayer of the prisoner; kindly of heart when one calleth to him. He who rescueth the fearful from the oppressor, who judgeth between the miserable and the strong.

Some similarities have been noted between this Hymn to Amun and the famous Hymn to the Sun from El-Amarna. This contains the basic tenets of the exclusive sun-worship which Pharaoh Akhenaten attempted to introduce towards the end of the Eighteenth dynasty, and to which we shall return in a later chapter. Both hymns refer to the god's goodness and his loving and creative nature and stress his support not only of the Egyptians but of the other peoples of the world –

Atum, who created mankind, who distinguished their nature and made their life; who made the colours different, one from the other.

The cult of Amen-Re was never exclusive in the same way as the solar cult of Akhenaten, and other gods and goddesses continued to be worshipped throughout Egypt alongside Amen-Re, but the Hymn is explicit about the supremacy of Amen-Re. The god is referred to as –

Sole One and Only, without peer, who presideth in Thebes, the Heliopolitan, the first of the *ennead*, who liveth daily on Truth.

In this passage, the unique nature of the god and his close association with the concept of truth are features which were developed in the solar cult of Akhenaten.

Apart from the myths and legends and the hymns, much can be learnt about the nature of Re by studying the rituals. All the main rituals were based on the Heliopolitan doctrine and were derived from the practices of the Old Kingdom. The sun-god was believed to die each night and to emerge each morning from the ocean, in the eastern horizon, re-born and re-invigorated. As the influence of the sun-god increased from the Fourth dynasty onwards, all the important deities became identified, to some extent, with Re. Elements from the Heliopolitan doctrine permeated their cults, and rituals performed for these gods came to include the lustration which the sun-god was thought to undergo each morning. In this solar baptism, the sun-god passed through the waters of the ocean, before being re-born and emerging purified and revitalized. The ritual baptism symbolized this event and renewed the life and vigour of the recipient, providing one of the greatest blessings of solar worship. In scenes where such rites are depicted, streams of water are shown passing over the recipient; the water is made up of a continuous flow of small hieroglyphic signs each in the form of the 'ankh' which symbolized life. Purification or the offering of a libation became an essential rite in all the important rituals and the recipient received re-birth through the medium of the water.

All except one of the rites which developed out of the Helipolitan liturgy were directed towards the king; he was the son of the sun-god and the chief priest and it was essential that he underwent this purification. Before he attended the god each morning, the king participated in a ritual which was known as the 'rite of the House of the Morning'. Each temple had a *Pr-Dw3t* ('House of the Morning'), where the king would be prepared for his meeting with the god. His toilet would commence at dawn. It would have been carried out for him only in the main temple of the chief state god, although, in theory, the king was present to perform the ritual in every temple throughout Egypt. He would be sprinkled with water by two priests who represented the gods Thoth and Horus. The water was brought from the Sacred Lake of the temple, for Nile water was believed to possess magical properties; it was regarded as the body fluid of the god Osiris. The solar liturgy was the basis of all later rituals, but elements of the Osirian doctrine also permeated the rites, and here both the essence of the sacred water and the two gods chosen to sprinkle the king, Horus and Thoth, (who had played important roles in revitalizing Osiris in the myth) have close associations with the Osirian doctrine.

Osiris and Re had certain similarities – both were nature gods, and both experienced regular renewal and resurrection from a state of death. Both cults played a part in the rite of the House of the Morning, in which the king achieved the renewal of life and youth and the gift of good fortune and was also identifed with Osiris whose members were revived by washing after death. The king was then fumigated with incense, given natron to chew which would purify his mouth, dressed and anointed; a ritual which must have closely resembled the Heliopolitan toilet performed for the early kings. The king was now ready to enter the god's temple and to perform the Daily Temple Ritual.

The ritual act of washing the king came to symbolize new life and immortality and it was performed for the king not only in the rite of the House of the Morning but also in the coronation and jubilee festivals. The meaning and significance of this baptism is brought out clearly in an inscription of a wall-scene found in the great hypostyle hall at Karnak, where King Sethos I is being purified with water by Horus and Seth; it reads –

I purify thee with life and dominion, that thou mayest grow young, like thy father Re, and make a jubilee-festival like Atum, being arisen gloriously as prince of joy.

Purification also occurred in the funerary liturgy when the daily bathing of the sun-god was repeated in the washing of the dead king's body for burial. Although originally an exclusively royal preparation, the funerary ritual eventually became available to all, and in addition to its solar associations, the water used in washing was thought to become the fluid of Osiris' own body which flowed through the body of the deceased and revived him.

Also associated with the dead and based on the solar cult was the ceremony of the Opening of the Mouth. This was performed on the mummy of the deceased on the day of interment and included rites of purification, censing and touching various parts of the body with an adze, to revitalize the corpse for eternity. The essential feature of this ritual was the belief that it would 'bring to life' by means of magic an inanimate object – whether it was a corpse, a statue, a model, or a figure carved or painted on the wall. It was probably first used on the statue of the dead king to imbue the inanimate form with the qualities, characteristics and abilities of the original. The ritual came to be used on non-royal funerary statuettes and models and also on the wall-scenes in the temples as well as those in the tombs. The form of the ritual was very similar to that of the Daily Temple Ritual, but whereas the Daily Temple Ritual was carried out on a number of occasions each day, the ceremony of the Opening of the Mouth was probably only used in the temples on special days for the consecration of the temple when it was handed over to its god, or the annual re-dedication of the temple and its contents at the festival on New Year's Day.

The rites mentioned so far were all performed for the king, or for the deceased. However, one ritual – the Daily Temple Ritual – was carried out on behalf of the god. The rite of the House of the Morning represented the daily morning lustration of the sun-god; similarly, the Daily Temple Ritual, performed for all temple deities, was based on the service originally devoted to Re in his temple at Heliopolis. The daily ritual which was offered to the state deities in the temples of the New Kingdom reflected features of the daily toilet of the sun-god and the death and resurrection of Osiris. By the Eighteenth dynasty the outward form of the ritual remained solar, but various elements present in the rites had taken on an Osirian significance.

Thus, the basis of all main Egyptian rituals was the solar toilet with its ritual cleansing of the god or king, followed by the offering of food. The use of water became essential – it revitalized the recipient and rendered him fit to perform the divine ritual. The act of baptism enabled the recipient to achieve the state of purity and near-divinity necessary to enter the god's presence. Washing became important not only in the rituals, but also as a religious duty which was observed and carried out in the Sacred Lake by the priests before they entered the temples. It is possible that the Egyptian later came to regard the cleansing of the skin as a means of absolving himself from sin, but the original significance of washing was based on the solar doctrine.

This summarizes the wide range of material on which our knowledge of the sun-cult is based. However, although the nature and mythology of the god are complex and frequently confusing, all sources show the most important characteristic of Re to be his ability to renew his strength and vitality, even after death, and to help others to achieve re-birth through the medium of specific rituals.

# 6 Mansions of the Ka

Throughout the period of development in pyramid-building, the burial customs of commoners followed a different course. These customs achieved great importance after the end of the Old Kingdom and we should now consider their religious background.

An important factor was the fundamental concept of the human personality. It was complex and consisted of at least five different elements in addition to the body. These included an individual's name (knowledge of which enabled a man's enemies to do him harm) and his shadow which was believed to enable him to procreate. There were also three immortal elements, possessed at first only by the gods, then by the king, and finally inherited by all men. One of these elements – the *ba* – was depicted as a human-headed bird. It was regarded as an animating force which may have corresponded in some respects to the Christian concept of the soul. Unlike the body which was confined to the tomb, the *ba* could fly to places which the deceased had formerly visited in life. The second element *akh* was a supernatural power which is difficult to interpret in modern terms; it seems to have been attained only after death. The third element was the *ka*, often depicted as a pair of upraised arms. No one satisfactory explanation of this power has been given, and the Egyptians seem to have used the word with different meanings in different contexts. Various interpretations have suggested that it was the double of its owner, or the embodiment of the vital force in living things, or the personification of abstract qualities and characteristics which make up the 'self' or personality of an individual. Again, we do not know exactly how the Egyptian was affected by his *ka* during his lifetime, but after death the *ka* can perhaps be regarded as a man's spirit – the part of him which ensured his immortality as an individual.

At death, the Egyptians believed that the insubstantial part of this complex personality separated itself from the body and was free to travel at will, but that it still preserved a link with the body in the tomb. A king's immortality could continue either by accompanying the sun in the heavens or by identification with Osiris, and ordinary people continued into eternity by travelling in the Osirian underworld – but the spirit still depended upon the body and the food offerings left at the tomb for its sustenance in the next life. Therefore, every effort was made to ensure that the body remained intact and that it retained as close a likeness as possible to the deceased. It was hoped that tomb robbers and evil spirits could be deterred by various architectural devices within the tomb and by magical formulae, but the actual preservation of the body was a complicated procedure. The technique is referred to today as 'mummification'. In fact, the words 'mummy' and 'mummification' are not derived from an ancient Egyptian source, but come from a Persian word *mummia*, meaning 'bitumen'. The Persians greatly prized a black bituminous exudation which occurred in certain areas by oozing from the ground. They believed it could cure certain ailments and gave it the name *mummia*. The embalmed bodies of the Egyptians from the Ptolemaic period onwards frequently had a blackened appearance; and so the bodies were wrongly thought to provide an alternative source of the medicinal bituminous material and the name *mummia* was applied to them. Regardless of the mistaken origin of this name, it was henceforth used to describe the embalmed bodies of ancient Egypt, and its usage has persisted over the centuries until the present day.

We know how the bodies of the deceased were at first naturally desiccated in Egypt by the effect of the heat and of the dry sand in which they were buried, and how increasingly sophisticated brick-lined tombs built for royalty and the nobility resulted in the rapid decomposition of the body. In these early dynasties, there were apparently unsuccessful attempts to preserve the body by applying dehydrating salts to the body's surface to remove moisture before decomposition could occur. However, the method generally adopted throughout the earliest dynasties and, for the nobility, throughout most of the Old Kingdom, was the building up in cloth and stucco-plaster of the bodily contours on a skeletal frame. The discovery of a canopic chest at Gizeh in the tomb of Queen Hetepheres, mother of Cheops, which contained the queen's mummified viscera, indicated that complete mummification involving evisceration and dehydration was being carried out, at least for royalty, in the Fourth dynasty. By the end of the Old Kingdom, use of this process was probably extended to the nobility.

Information concerning the various stages in this process is limited. Mummified bodies from later periods provide some evidence, but ancient Egyptian texts do not give any complete record of the various techniques involved. The best account of mummification which we possess comes from the Greeks who wrote about Egypt – Herodotus in the Fifth century BC and Diodorus Siculus about four hundred years later. Although they recorded this information thousands of years after the end of the Old Kingdom, the basic process remained the same, with the later introduction of certain elaborations. Herodotus describes three methods apparently in use at his time, but the most expensive of these was obviously based on the method devised to preserve the royal bodies of the Old Kingdom. Except for the heart (which was believed to be the seat of the intellect and of the emotions) and the kidneys, the viscera were removed from the body by making an incision in the right side of the abdomen. They were cleaned, treated with natron and placed in a canopic chest or box. At later periods, they were sometimes wrapped in packages and replaced in the bodily cavities, or they were stored in vessels known as 'canopic jars'. There were four of these to a set, usually made of stone, and each was dedicated to one of the 'Four Sons of Horus'. In the New Kingdom, the stoppers of the jars were carved to represent these demi-gods – the ape-headed Hapy, the jackal-headed Duamutef, the hawk-headed Qebhsenuef, and the human-headed Imset.

After evisceration, the body was cleansed and rinsed, and the cavities were filled with various spices. The body was then preserved by rapid dehydration, so that decomposition would be arrested. To replace the desiccating effect of the sand in the original burial-pit, natron was used as a dehydrating agent. The dispute today is whether the body was actually immersed and soaked in a bath of natron or whether it was packed in a bed of dry natron. Recent experiments suggest that the second method was more commonly used. This process took between forty and seventy days. The body was finally washed again, and strips of fine linen bandaging, treated with a gummy adhesive substance were bound tightly around the body. The body was finally removed from the embalmer's workshop, and was probably taken to the house of the deceased, before being transported to the tomb.

During the New Kingdom, various advances were made in this process, which are well displayed in the two caches of royal mummies found at Thebes between AD1881 and 1898. Various methods of removing the brain were employed, the most common one being to force an instrument up the nostril and through the intervening bone structure. The brain was then removed, perhaps using a kind of ladle, and resin-soaked strips of linen were packed into the skull cavity. Towards the end of the Eighteenth dynasty, an operation was introduced which was to become increasingly evident during the Twenty-first dynasty. Attempts were made to restore the lifelike contours of the body of Amenophis III, an elderly and obese ruler, by subcutaneous packing. By the Twenty-first dynasty, mummification had reached its peak and techniques attempted to reproduce the lifelike contours and facial appearance of the deceased. A series of small incisions was made in the surface of the skin, through which packing was inserted. The neck and cheeks were also packed, with the face stuffing being introduced through the mouth. Artificial eyes were placed in the eye sockets, the face and often the whole body painted with ochre, and the natural tresses were augmented with false plaits and curls.

A decline in standards is evident from the Twenty-second dynasty, and subcutaneous packing ceased to be used. With a continuing decline in religious beliefs, mummification ceased to have a deep religious significance and became an expensive and commercial exercise. This is particularly true of the mummies of the Ptolemaic and Roman periods, when the bodies are usually poorly preserved inside their gilded and painted cartonnage cases. Mummification continued until the Christian era, when elaborate outer wrappings but superficial treatment of the body signified the final stage of this ancient practice. The Moslem invasion of Egypt in AD641 and the subsequent conversion of many of the Egyptians to Islam meant the end of mummification as a method of preserving the bodies of the dead.

However, we now return to the period when this process was an essential feature of Egyptian funerary beliefs and the correct environment was provided for the mummy and the deceased's continued existence after death. Throughout the Old Kingdom, the mastaba type of tomb was used for the burial of the nobility, although rock-cut tombs, introduced at Gizeh during the Fourth dynasty, gained popularity. These maintained the outward appearance of the mastaba tomb but the associated offering chapels were excavated from the solid rock to allow a greater area for wall decoration. Towards the end of the Old Kingdom, it became increasingly common for the provincial nobility to prepare tombs for themselves in the desert cliffs of their own provinces. However, the traditional mastaba tomb continued to have two main functional parts – the underground burial chamber and the stairway or shaft which provided access, and the superstructure which marked and protected the burial. By the Old Kingdom, two other features – the chapel and the *serdab*, included for the presentation of offerings, – become associated with the superstructure. The typical early Old Kingdom burial site is well-illustrated at Saqqara, Dahshur, Medum, Abusir and Gizeh, where the mastaba tombs belonging to the royal family and the court officials are found grouped around the pyramids of the kings. Various innovations occurred even in this traditional form of burial place. In the Fourth dynasty, the proximity of the court at Memphis to the fine limestone quarries at Tura and the presence of so many skilful craftsmen in the area, attracted by the royal court, resulted in the gradual replacement of brick by stone in these tombs, especially to face the walls of the offering chamber. Also, a deeper burial chamber was built, reached by means of a larger stairway or passage, and eventually, a new access was provided in the form of a vertical pit. A second shaft and burial chamber were also often incorporated in the structure for the tomb-owner's wife. The security and impregnability of the tomb was increased by blocking the doors within the substructure with stone or brick, and by filling the access shafts with gravel or rock. The superstructure was now made either of a solid masonry core or of rubble which was contained within solid walls. It had an outer facing of smooth limestone.

The earliest offering chapels were attached to the outside of the tombs, adjacent to the east wall. These were open 'enclosures', built of brick, and placed in front of the southern stela. Such stelae, set in the east wall, gave the name and titles of the tomb owner together with the appropriate offering formulae. Gradually, a flat

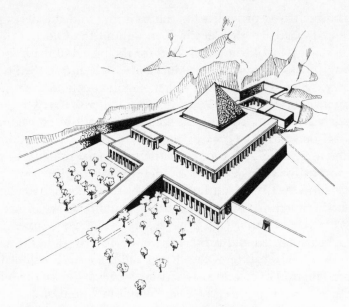

Figure 24 The funerary Temple of Nebhepetre Mentuhotep –
a reconstruction

or vaulted roof and a doorway were added to the chapel, probably
to protect the inner wall surfaces from damage caused by robbers
or the weather. A vestibule and portico, several offering chambers
and storerooms were also included. From the Fourth dynasty
onwards, the superstructure also contained a *serdab* (a chamber to
which the modern Arabic word meaning 'cellar' has been applied).
A statue of the deceased and also sometimes of his family were
placed in the *serdab*, although this only became customary in the
Fifth dynasty. The *serdab* was an enclosed room with no doors or
windows. A narrow hole or slit was made in one wall, opposite the
eye-level of the statue inside. The statue served as a substitute for
the tomb-owner's mummy which was vulnerable and easily
destroyed; another safeguard in some tombs was the provision of
a 'reserve head' which was placed in the burial chamber; this was a
likeness of the tomb-owner's face and head made in a durable
material. It was possibly a gift made by the king to a favoured
courtier. The *serdab* – essentially a secret and inaccessible room
within the superstructure, designed to provide the statue with the
utmost protection – was later often attached to the public offering
area of the tomb.

The mummified body and the tomb were believed to be

essential to the continued existence of their owner after death. However, this was not guaranteed unless the ritual was properly performed and all material provisions were made in the tomb for the hereafter. The provisioning of a man's tomb with food and drink was mainly the duty of his heir and of his descendants. When performed for several generations of ancestors this became an onerous duty and consequently was frequently neglected after a passage of time had elapsed since the tomb-owner's death. The regular supply of fresh provisions placed on a flat altar table in the tomb-chapel was so important for the sustenance and well-being of the ka of the deceased that other methods of insurance against spiritual starvation had to be employed. One way was to enter into a contract with a ka-priest. This man and his descendants were paid in kind, with the produce from a piece of land set aside by the tomb-owner or by the king, on his behalf, for this purpose. In return, the priest made regular offerings of food at the owner's tomb; the priest's descendants inherited the income and the obligation to the tomb, and theoretically, the ka-endowment guaranteed the eternal sustenance of one's ka. However, it soon became apparent that such agreements lapsed after a period of time and the Egyptians were obliged to consider other methods which did not rely on human honesty.

We have seen that the tomb was regarded as the 'House of the Ka', where the dead man's spirit could retain a locality on earth to which it could return to receive sustenance. Only the kings and possibly some of the queens were buried in pyramids, and the nobles built and stocked their mastaba tombs, grouped either around the royal pyramids, or in separate 'cities of the dead'. The life after death was expected to reflect a man's existence in this world, except it was hoped that it would be free from worry, danger and illness. In addition to the Osirian and solar concepts of the afterlife, the most commonly held belief was that a man would pass his eternity in his tomb, with access to the pastimes and possessions of his successful earthly existence. Although decorative art and crafts played a part in everyday life, the impetus for the progress made in statuary, wall reliefs and paintings came from their use in tomb decoration and funerary equipment, as magical substitutes to assist the dead. In the Old Kingdom, the decoration of the walls and the contents of the tomb were designed to provide the dead man with the idealized afterlife he expected. Many aspects of his life were depicted; his wife and family; servants;

home; clothing; hobbies such as hunting, fishing and fowling; and features of his career, showing his power and influence. The accompanying inscriptions conferred material benefits on the tomb-owner, or provided spells to protect him against evil spirits and dangers which might impede his progress into the next world, or against the constant threat of tomb-robbers. The tomb-owner was himself represented in the tomb by various substitutes – the mummified body or his 'reserve head', or a full-size statue, or the

Figure 25 Part of a mural decoration showing the god Osiris; from the tomb of Sennedjem, Thebes. 19th dynasty

carved and painted likenesses in the wall-reliefs. Domestic articles were also placed in the tomb; the dryness of the climate preserving them to a remarkable degree, so that we have inherited a wealth of information concerning the everyday lives of the well-to-do Egyptians. However, the most important provision was of course food and drink, and these were originally supplied with varying degrees of reliability by the tomb-owner's family heirs or his *ka*-priest. Another solution to this problem was to ensure that, in the tomb, there were scenes of food-production and the presentation of offerings, which could supply the deceased's needs if the other methods failed. So, scenes of harvesting, slaughtering, brewing and baking were placed on the tomb walls in addition to an offering list and magical formulae to grant the tomb-owner an abundance of food.

A biography of the deceased, in which his achievements were listed, was also included on the tomb wall; this established his name, ownership of the tomb, his family, his *ka*-priest and his rank. This, presumably, would grant him equal status in the next life, and would also impress visitors to his tomb with his success and importance.

It was believed that the transformation of the tomb-reliefs and contents from substitutes into real people and objects, was brought about by the potent magic of the mortuary service. Before burial, the ritual of 'Opening the Mouth' was performed on the mummy of the deceased. The priest would touch the mouth of the mummy with an instrument so that it could speak and eat the funerary meal, so that its nose could smell again and its eyes could see. Similarly, the members of his family and servants, represented in the wall scenes or by tomb statuettes, would come to life. The model boat which formed part of the tomb equipment would become a full-size vessel in which he could sail on the Nile. All the other people and activities shown in the wall-scenes would also become real not just momentarily, but for eternity, to provide company or to add to the happiness of the tomb-owner.

In the Fourth dynasty, the scenes in the tombs at Gizeh were generally limited to the outer rooms of the chapel and were not usually placed in the offering room. In the early part of the Fifth dynasty, the decoration remained simple and the subject matter was similar to that depicted in the previous dynasty. However, in the second part of the Fifth dynasty, the interior of the chapels became more complex, and included many more rooms. There is little evidence of reliefs in provincial tombs before the Fifth dynasty but the provincial nomarchs of the Fifth and Sixth dynasties adopted the design of the decorated rock-cut tombs which originated at Gizeh towards the end of the Fourth dynasty. They transferred this style to the cliffs at the edge of the desert, near their provincial capital cities. In the Sixth dynasty, the mastaba tombs in the neighbourhood of Teti's pyramid at Saqqara show the development of multiple-roomed chapels which occupy a large area of the interior of the superstructure. In the tomb of Mereruka at Saqqara – the finest of this type – a whole series of apartments was provided for the tomb-owner, his wife and his son. The walls of the burial chamber were now decorated with scenes; including lists of food, funerary equipment, details of the owner and his family, and everyday activities. The painted burial chamber was retained in the rock-cut tombs of Upper Egypt, at the end of the Old Kingdom and into the First Intermediate period. In the Sixth dynasty and the succeeding period, the provincial reliefs showed the persistence of two general trends – the old Memphite traditions continued in certain areas, but with a diminishing standard of excellence, while elsewhere a second style developed – more angular and cruder than the Memphite style – which was used in the poorer tombs.

However, it was the traditional Memphite style of the Old Kingdom which set a pattern for the decoration of later tombs. In other civilizations, art has been used to decorate and to beautify buildings, but Egyptian religious art was not intended for this purpose; neither did it seek to inspire spiritually or to commemorate great deeds or rulers. The scenes were there in the tombs and in the temples to sustain and preserve life. They imitated aspects of life as closely as possible but with certain limitations. Egyptian tomb art can be compared with other primitive art in that it attempts to provide a diagram of what is known to exist and what the artist wishes to 'come into being'; but it is not the artist's personal view. This basic concept was carried to extremes in Egyptian religious art and produced some apparently bizarre portrayals of the human figure and an almost total disregard for the laws of perspective. To fully appreciate their tomb art, it is essential to learn to 'read' the scenes in correct order and to be aware of the religious principles which fettered their art.

Perhaps because the climate and geography of Egypt induced a sense of permanence and stability in its inhabitants, the Egyptians

13 Section of papyrus of Hent-Taui, musician-priestess of Amen-Re. The deceased and Thoth (in form of baboon) worship the sun-disc which contains Eye of Re. XXI Dynasty. British Museum

14 Papyrus of Pa-Shebut-Mut. The deceased and her soul in worship; Shu holds aloft disc of the sun; below, four rudders of heaven. British Museum

15 Temple of Karnak – scarabeus
on plinth, near Sacred Lake

16 Mummy held upright by Anubis
at entrance to tomb, for Opening of the Mou[
From *Book of the Dead*,
Papyrus of Hunefer. British Museum.

17 Bronze statuette of
Isis suckling Horus

18 Bronze head of Osiris

19 Model boat from tomb

20 Model boat from tomb

21 Wooden chest containing canopic jars and viscera

22 Ushabti-figure

23 Ushabti-figure, finest type

24 Tomb model of servants carrying sedan chair

gave to their art a feeling of timelessness; they sought, above all else, to retain the forms and traditions established in the early periods. There were few attempts to produce new and different styles in religious art until the revolution in art forms during the Amarna period at the end of the Eighteenth dynasty, to which we shall return in Chapter eight. The statuary evokes a feeling of serenity and stability; in the wall scenes, great attention was paid to detail, but the scenes were not intended to stir the emotions. Background scenery was usually indicated by a representative tree or strip of Nile water; it is as if a plan or outline of the terrain is being given, against which the humans and animals act out their parts. The figures are stylized with little or no personality, and merely play a set role. Originality was not required from the artist and there was no desire to improve upon the work of previous artists – the aim was to recapture as nearly as possible the perfection of early traditional art, which later generations believed to have originated in the Old Kingdom. The finest examples of Egyptian art do, however, show a degree of originality, but only in the skilful execution of a particular statue or wall relief; the style and concept of the work are still in the tradition imposed by religious belief and custom. Indeed, the artist was usually

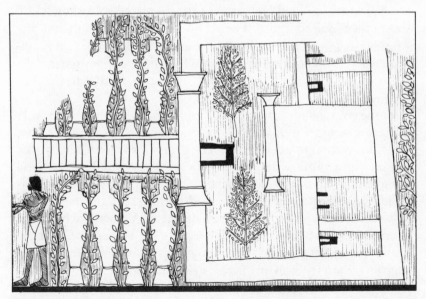

Figure 26 A garden and villa – from a mural painting in the tomb of Min-nakht at Thebes. 18th dynasty, reign of Tuthmosis III

anonymous, an official of the state who performed his task in the same way as his fellow craftsmen – the quarrymen, carpenters, stone-masons, and metal-smiths. He worked as a member of a team, employed by the king to equip and furnish the tomb, and, at the royal pleasure, to do the same for members of the royal family, and for privileged courtiers. His apprenticeship to a master artist would have involved copying earlier forms and acquiring basic and repetitive skills. The master would direct his team in decorating the tomb, and certain tasks would be allotted to each man.

In the Old Kingdom, the necropolises were situated in areas where the local stone was of excellent quality, and therefore the tomb scenes were carved in low relief on limestone walls, and then painted. Preliminary sketches of the wall decoration were prepared and, subject to the owner's approval, the scenes were then transferred to the walls from the papyrus, and outlined in ink, before the reliefs were carved. This was done in bas-relief, so that the figures and objects stood out from the background which had been chiselled away. Finally, the reliefs were painted in vivid colours and the details were highlighted. It is a feature of Egyptian art that the figures were drawn according to certain measurements, so that there was the same distance between various points on the body – nose to chin, shoulders to waist and so forth – and these proportions could be increased or decreased according to the size of the required figure. The preliminary sketch and the outline drawing made on the wall included guide-lines (in the Old Kingdom) or a complete grid (in the New Kingdom) which assisted the artist to position the figures and to draw them in correct proportion.

In the completed wall composition of the Old Kingdom tomb, the size of a figure indicated his status; it was not an attempt to put the composition in perspective. The tomb-owner was always the largest figure; his wife was a little smaller, and his sons and daughters, even if they had reached adulthood, were still shown as children, characteristically nude and with the plait of hair at the side of the head – known as the 'Sidelock of Youth' – which was worn until puberty. Subordinates, such as servants, farm-labourers, and craftsmen, were shown on a smaller scale, often in registers, indicating their relative insignificance. They were present in the tomb only to assist the tomb-owner. Sometimes, the registers also show a sequence of events with inscriptions to record the remarks and conversation of the figures. Because of the limited wall area in a tomb, it was also necessary to save space, and therefore a crowd was represented by three people.

The principal characters – the tomb-owner and his family – exhibit certain features which are immediately distinctive and often physically impossible. They are inevitably shown as young adults, in perfect health and with indistinguishable and 'idealized' faces, which represent the ancient Egyptian concept of physical beauty. Such a figure is depicted in a stiff, formalized pose; his head is in profile and one eye is shown but this is painted frontally with the pupil and iris in the centre. Again, the body from the shoulders to the edge of the torso is shown frontally, but only one breast is indicated, while the legs and the feet are shown in profile, so that although the figure appears to be moving towards the left or right, the eye and torso face the viewer. This strange and unlikely stance reflects, yet again, the magical and practical aspects of the art. The Egyptians, in painting what they knew to exist, attempted to show as many parts of the body as possible, so that the tomb-owner and his family would have full use of them, once they had been brought to life by means of magic. If the figures had been drawn in perspective, with the nose and feet and legs shown frontally, and consequently foreshortened and flattened, then their correct functions could not have been fulfilled in the next world. Similarly, the torso and arms were shown frontally so that they could be used with maximum strength and the eye was fully depicted to provide perfect sight.

The concept of 'what is depicted in the wall scenes can be brought to life when required' was extended further. The contents of dishes and baskets are shown piled high; a diagrammatic section is provided of the river Nile, complete with teeming fish; houses and buildings, lakes and gardens are also represented in a diagrammatic form.

The Egyptians retained these artistic conventions because of their religious concepts, but other secular art forms and even occasionally the representations in tomb art of animals and unimportant persons – such as servants or workers – break away from the strict religious requirements, and show us that the Egyptian artists were quite capable of drawing and painting naturalistically and with vigour, when they were free from restrictions.

Generally, although variations were introduced in the later dynasties, and no two tombs were identical, the type of scene found in the nobleman's tomb of the Old Kingdom became a standard form of decoration. This includes those we can classify as offering scenes, those showing life on the owner's country estate: agricultural pursuits, harvesting, herding cattle, marshalling wild and domestic animals, dairying, and bird-netting; the pastimes of the tomb-owner, such as hunting birds and spearing fish in a papyrus swamp, or hunting wild animals in the desert. Also, the various stages in his funeral occupy a section of the wall space, and frequently, scenes are included which show the craftsmen at work, preparing equipment for his tomb or funerary procession.

The seemingly stable and secure society which enabled such elaborate tombs to be built was not destined to survive. The Sixth dynasty saw a general decline in the power and wealth of the monarchy and the final dissolution of the political, economic and religious structure of the Old Kingdom began to take effect from the end of the reign of Pepy II. A period of disorder and disillusionment followed, when the beliefs and ideals of the Egyptians were severely tested. Despite the apparent wealth and prosperity of the Sixth dynasty and Egypt's increased influence in Asia Minor and Nubia, the seeds of ultimate destruction were already present in society and in the administration. The factors which contributed to the fall of the king and the government of the Old Kingdom were partly social and economic but also religious; they were rooted in traditions which had been handed down since the Fourth dynasty.

At first, the chasm which had existed between the king and his subjects was assiduously maintained. He married a close relative; all important administrative posts were awarded to members of the royal family; his burial-place was a pyramid which was surrounded by the greatly inferior mastaba tombs of his courtiers who wished to be near him in death as they had been in life. His bounty alone ensured that his nobles and officials could aspire to tombs provisioned with funerary goods. However, various factors contributed to the ultimate bridging of this gap between the king and his subjects; he eventually became just one of many local rulers who exercised power over a limited area, and in the chaos which followed the collapse of the Old Kingdom, there was a return to the political situation which had existed prior to the unification of Egypt.

The economic and political actions of the kings over a period of hundreds of years had disastrous results, and there was a gradual equalization of wealth from the Fourth dynasty onwards. The

Figure 27 Mural painting from the tomb of Ramose at Thebes, showing attendants carrying funerary furniture during the tomb-owner's funerary procession. 18th dynasty, reign of Amenophis III

Figure 28 Painting from the tomb of Arinefer at Thebes, showing the *Ba* (soul) of the deceased as a human-headed bird and his shadow in front of the tomb's entrance. Ramesside period

king, in theory, was the sole owner of Egypt and all its inhabitants and assets, but gradually, the royal resources were depleted. Gifts of crown land to favoured nobles enabled them to provision their tombs and to retain their *ka*-priests, but the royal domains were proportionately decreased; with a widening circle of inheritance, the land was broken down into increasingly small units. The king also made gifts of tombs to favoured nobles. The land thus given was usually free from taxation and was cultivated in order to provide food for the noble's tomb and to pay the priest who attended this tomb. Such exemptions, in force from the Fourth dynasty, were published as royal decrees.

The pyramid complexes and their funerary endowments were also built and maintained at royal expense, and each king was required not only to build his own pyramid and feed his mortuary priesthood and their families, but also to maintain the pyramids and priests of previous rulers. This became an onerous task. In addition, the possessions and personnel of the pyramid mortuary temples were exempt from taxation and enforced labour drafts. Gradually, the king's once huge resources were drained and were not replenished. The economic situation was reflected in the pyramids themselves, for, although pyramids continued to be built during the Fifth and Sixth dynasties, with complexes constructed along traditional lines, they were built of inferior materials. Many of the finest craftsmen were now employed in constructing and decorating the increasing number of tombs belonging to the nobility.

The increased importance of the nobility and the parallel decline in royal power is seen most clearly in their burial places. The royal pyramids became smaller and the building materials inferior, the tombs of the nobles became larger and more complex, with an increasing number of beautifully executed wall-reliefs. The diminishing economic power of the royal family prompted the king to marry outside his circle of close relatives, and to take a wife from the now wealthy nobility. From the end of the Fourth dynasty, there was an increasing number of marriages between the kings and their non-royal subjects. The myth of the king's divinity, his special relationship with the gods, the divinity of his heir, and the difference between the royal family and their subjects could no longer be fully sustained. By the Fifth dynasty, appointment to high position was no longer reserved for a member of the royal family; many officials were now of non-royal origin. The local governorships which had first been granted as a special sign of the king's favour, and on a temporary basis, now became hereditary and were no longer dependent on the king's will. These nomarchs came to regard their positions as a rightful inheritance rather than an honour bestowed by the king, and, often isolated in areas many miles from Memphis and the Court, they became increasingly independent of centralized government and of the king. Economically and politically, they no longer felt committed to the king. At first, he tried to win their loyalty by granting them titles and by choosing the vizier from amongst the provincial nobility, thus also hoping to stem the ambition of the nomarchs at Memphis, but his inability to rule them by means of force or by gifts and titles was all too soon apparent. Both the nobles at the capital and those in the provinces became a real threat to royal supremacy. This was shown in the burial customs of the Sixth dynasty, when the tombs of the nobility no longer clustered around the base of the king's pyramid, in the hope of obtaining a vicarious afterlife for the deceased. Increased in size and complexity as befitted the independence of the owners, the tombs of the provincial nobility were now situated near to the chief towns of their administrative areas, where they had come to exercise almost princely powers.

The king faced yet another direct threat to his absolute authority. The endowments and privileges of tax exemption which were enjoyed by the nobility and the funerary establishments were gradually extended to the temples of the gods. These cult centres and their personnel also became increasingly independent, and of these, the cult and priesthood of Re took control. The sun-god's priesthood had come to exercise great influence over the king and Re had been adopted as the great state god. By the Fifth dynasty, the relative importance of Re is reflected by the king's adoption of the title 'son of Re', implying royal subordination to the god. The king was no longer a divine equal, but merely the son and heir of the sun-god. We have seen that, in the Fifth dynasty, resources were diverted from building the king's pyramids to the construction of magnificent temples dedicated to the sun. By the Sixth dynasty, such solar temples no longer seem to have been built, although this was probably due to economic rather than religious factors.

The king was threatened from all sides; for several generations, the cumulative effects of these policies had been at work, undermining the king's position and the centralized government. The final collapse of the Old Kingdom was probably precipitated by a further decline in royal power brought about by the long reign of Pepy II, whose rule of over ninety years must have provided a timely opportunity for the dissident factions to take advantage of a weak and elderly ruler. The external security of the country was also threatened by the continuing infiltration of Beduin nomads into Egypt on the north-eastern border. Finally, the system collapsed, or, perhaps more accurately, disintegrated, leaving a state of chaos and confusion which lasted for many years.

This period of political, social and economic dissolution is referred to by historians as the First Intermediate period; it spans the Seventh to the Tenth dynasties, although the Eleventh dynasty is also sometimes included under this heading. The Seventh and the Eighth dynasties were marked by general chaos, and by the disintegration of the centralized government at Memphis where, although an attempt was apparently made to retain some semblance of authority, more and more concessions were made to provincial rulers. The land of Egypt was once again split into many different principalities, each under a local ruler – a situation which resembled the early Predynastic divisions. Internal disorder was exacerbated by border attacks and probably by some degree of infiltration by the Beduin nomads.

The end of accepted traditions and religious values forced the Egyptians into a state of self-examination. The social collapse of the country brought about a period of chaos when law and order were no longer upheld, when vandals and thieves roamed the countryside, and when famine and economic depression resulted from the breakdown of the previously carefully maintained irrigation system.

Two Egyptian texts provide a vivid account of the calamity which overtook the country and of men's reactions to these events. The first – the so-called 'Admonitions of a prophet' – probably reflects conditions at the end of the Sixth dynasty; it tells how danger threatens Egypt from within and without. Foreign mercenary troops rise against the government and officialdom is threatened by the people; the Beduin provide an external threat on Egypt's eastern border. The ruler – almost certainly the aged king Pepy II who reigned at the end of the Sixth dynasty – remains oblivious to the dangers, in the safety of his palace. A wise man, Ipuwer, appears at Court, and tells of the dangers already threatening, and urges that an attempt is made to combat them. He describes a situation in which the order of the Old Kingdom is completely reversed. The upper and lower classes find their positions changed – 'Nay, but the poor men now possess fine things. He who once made for himself no sandals now possesseth riches.'

Violence, robbery and murder are commonplace, and famine, disease and death are widespread – 'Nay, but the heart is violent. Plague stalketh through the land and blood is everywhere'. Gradually, the administration breaks down, and Egypt's trade with foreign lands, once so flourishing, now ceases. The people wish that they had never been born – 'Nay, but great and small say: "I wish I were dead!" Little children say: "He ought never to have caused me to live".'

However, even in death, there is no peace, for the materials for the elaborate burials are no longer to be found, and the tombs of the nobles are plundered and the bodies torn from the tombs. Finally, the kingship is completely destroyed, and the poor become rich at the expense of the rich – 'Behold, a thing hath been done that happened not aforetime; it is come to this that the king hath been taken away by poor men'.

In such a plight, it is not surprising that the Egyptians questioned their own existence, and even the continuation of life after death. This is expressed in the second text which is often referred to as 'The dispute with his soul of one who is tired of life.' A man, weary of his existence, decides to kill himself, but his soul – envisaged as a separate entity which can leave the man's side at death – decides to desert the man, because, without a tomb and a continuing supply of food, the soul will suffer hardship after his death. The poem is presented as a verbal conflict between the man and his soul. The man tries to persuade his soul to remain with him; he tells of the terrible conditions which prevail –

> To whom do I speak today?
> Brothers are evil,
> Friends of today, they are not lovable.

> To whom do I speak today?
> Men rob,
> Every man seizeth his neighbour's (goods).

> To whom do I speak today?
> The sin that smiteth the land,
> It hath no end.

Finally, he considers the benefits which death, by comparison, would bestow on him –

> Death is before me today,
> As when a sick man becometh whole,
> As when one walketh abroad after sickness.

> Death is before me today,
> As the odour of myrrh,
> As when one sitteth under the sail on a windy day.

> Death is before me today,
> As when a man longeth to see his house again
> After he has spent many years in captivity.

Eventually, the soul persuades the man not to invite death before his time, but to wait so that, in due course, they might have a resting place together.

This poem, one of the most famous in Egyptian literature, is interesting because it has a unique theme. In the earlier times of security and stability, man had not openly questioned his existence nor had he wished to contemplate suicide. Oppressed by the conditions around him his poem expresses despair and pessimism – emotions which are not generally found in Egyptian literature. During this period and the Middle Kingdom which followed, the content of the literature is generally more profound. Self-examination and self-awareness appear in the writings for the first time, and religious beliefs also undergo a great transformation. Outward materialistic expressions of piety are replaced by an increasing awareness of justice, charity and virtue. At the same time, sculpture, painting and the decoration of the tombs and temples indicate that there was a general decline in the standard of artistic craftsmanship.

The old order had disappeared and the exclusive concept of the royal afterlife which had dominated the beliefs of the Old Kingdom was no longer acceptable to the mass of the people. Gradually, everyone came to expect that his individual existence would continue after death and that this right would not be based on the power and influence of the king. First, the nobles, then those who could afford the expense of a tomb and its lavish equipment, and finally even the peasants came to aspire to an individual immortality. With this democratization of religious and funerary beliefs, the cult of the sun declined and the cult of Osiris emerged to exert an unprecedented influence over all classes of society.

Out of the chaotic conditions of the Seventh and Eighth dynasties, there eventually arose a powerful local family at Heracleopolis. These rulers, according to the history written hundreds of years later by the priest Manetho, formed the Ninth and Tenth dynasties. Some were named Akhtoy, and they restored some semblance of order to the country, particularly to the area between Memphis in the north and Thebes in the south – a region generally described as Middle Egypt. Here, the local princes enjoyed an era of comparative peace. Elaborate tombs were prepared and equipped for them in the cliffs at Beni Hasan, Akhmim and El-Bersha, in the vicinity of their own Courts.

In the meantime, in the south, Thebes was developing from a

small and insignificant village into a centre which would one day become the capital of Egypt. Here, a line of local princes who traced their ancestry to a nobleman named Inyotef the Great, were soon to raise their local town to a position of prominence. From this family of Theban princes there emerged a man who was to restore the unity of Egypt and to usher in the Middle Kingdom. Little is known of the successful campaigns of Nebhepetre Mentuhotep against the rulers of Heracleopolis, but his expansion northwards and southwards appears to have been gradual, and his break with the Heracleopolitan rulers came only towards the end of the conflict. Eventually, he brought Egypt again under one central control and, with his successors, established the Eleventh dynasty. A later inscription, dating to the Ramesside period, gives Menes (Narmer, of the First dynasty), Nebhepetre (of the Eleventh dynasty) and Amosis (of the Eighteenth dynasty) as the three founders of the greatest periods of Egypt's history.

A fitting monument to this king was provided by his unique tomb-temple situated adjacent to the cliffs at Deir el-Bahri. The rulers of the Seventh dynasty had arranged to be buried at south Saqqara, and the kings of the Ninth and Tenth dynasties were also probably buried in the ancient northern necropolis, but Nebhepetre Mentuhotep was buried near his own town, only a short distance from his predecessors' tombs. Here, against the magnificent backdrop of the Theban hills, and now adjacent to the later and much better preserved temple of Queen Hatshepsut of the Eighteenth dynasty, Mentuhotep's architects designed a building which was original and awe-inspiring in concept. The building included a pyramid of solid construction with a rubble core faced with limestone, a burial chamber for the king which was situated elsewhere in the complex, a funerary temple, and other areas associated with the celebration of the king's jubilee festival and for the burial of members of the royal Court. The overall design was never repeated in its entirety, and even the neighbouring temple built many generations later by Queen Hatshepsut's architect reflected only some of the more obvious features found in Mentuhotep's complex.

This king gradually restored Egypt's power, but little is known of his methods of administrating the country. He continued to reside at Thebes rather than moving back to the north. He did not suppress the provincial nobility, but may have adopted the custom previously in force in the early Old Kingdom of appointing the provincial nomarchs himself and of abolishing hereditary succession in these posts. The tombs of the nobles during this period show no evidence of upheaval or a break in the succession of the nomarchs, and Mentuhotep probably devised peaceful but effective methods of gaining the allegiance of these men.

He left a united and peaceful realm to his successors, S'ankhkare Mentuhotep II and Nebtowere Mentuhotep III. The next upheaval occurred when the vizier of Mentuhotep III, a man named Amenemhe, appears to have conspired against his master and seized the throne to become Amenemmes I, the founder of the Twelfth dynasty and one of Egypt's greatest kings.

Amenemmes I was of non-royal descent, and may have been born in southern Upper Egypt. His mother was an inhabitant of Elephantine, and his father, a commoner, was named Sesostris. It has been suggested that his statues show indications of Nubian blood in the strong and forceful features of his face. With no royal blood, and as an usurper of the throne, Amenemmes faced considerable problems, but his strength and determination equipped him for this challenge and he established one of the most dynamic and stable of all Egyptian dynasties. He transferred the capital city from Thebes to a new city in the north, named It-towy, which lay to the south of Memphis. Although many Theban artists were transferred to this city, many of the old associations with the south were lost and a fresh start was made. His pyramid was built at nearby Lisht and it was surrounded by the mastaba tombs and pit tombs of his nobles. This was a return to the Old Kingdom concept of building the nobles' tombs at the base of the king's pyramid, and reflected the new political situation. As a usurper, Amenemmes desperately needed the support of the nobles. Their allegiance was rewarded by the restoration of many of their former privileges, and new provincial governors were installed to replace those suppressed by the Mentuhoteps. Nevertheless the royal funerary temples at Thebes were still maintained by large priesthoods, and non-royal cemeteries in the vicinity were used for the burial of the priestly and official personnel who remained behind at the former capital. Many soldiers, priests, officials and courtiers, although they had accompanied the king to It-towy and had spent their working lives there, also elected to return to Thebes for burial. The country was now more easily governed from its northern capital, and Egypt once again flourished and prospered. The successors of Amenemmes I inherited a stable realm, and they carried out extensive programmes of construction and restoration of sacred buildings, re-established an efficient irrigation system and developed a successful system of land reclamation in the Fayoum basin. They traded with Byblos, Phoenecia, Crete and Punt, and conquered and colonized the Nubians to the south, building a string of great brick fortresses there to subdue the surrounding areas between the cataracts on the Nile. These ensured Egypt's access to the wealth of Nubia, particularly the gold, and eventually these fortresses became permanent with their own domestic quarters, temples and tombs.

However, these rulers faced internal problems and were apparently threatened in their supremacy by the local governors as the kings of the Old Kingdom had been, many years before. Unlike the Old Kingdom rulers, the kings of the Twelfth dynasty were strong enough to take decisive action to silence this threat forever. These nomarchs were able to hold courts in their provincial centres, and to build fine local tombs. They could raise their own troops and impose or remit taxation on their local subjects. Although the king closely supervised their activites and could demand both troops and ships from them, they were nevertheless a constant threat. By the reign of Sesostris III, they were once again causing problems for the king, and he deprived them of their rights and privileges. It is not certain how he achieved this end, but the nomarchs never again wielded significant power in Egypt. Future clashes would come between the king and the temple priesthoods but not between king and nomarchs. The local courts were closed down and the great provincial tombs were no longer built. A new administration was established which was directly responsible to the vizier and to the king. This new middle-class, raised from the craftsmen, tradesmen and small farmers, owed its newly established importance and its allegiance to the king.

Although, as we shall see, the cult of Re had very largely been replaced by those of Osiris and Amun, the kings of the Twelfth dynasty returned to the type of burial complex which had been built for the kings of the Old Kingdom. Amenemmes I built his pyramid at Lisht, near to his new capital. Although it was modest in size compared with the Old Kingdom complexes, and it incorporated certain Theban features, it owed much to the influence of the Old Kingdom concept. Sesostris I also built his pyramid at Lisht, although other kings of the dynasty chose other sites. Amenemmes II built his at Dahshur, and Sesostris II at

Illahun; Sesostris III constructed a pyramid at Dahshur and may also have built a cenotaph in the form of a mastaba tomb at Abydos. Amenemmes III had two pyramids, one at Dahshur and one at Hawara. These complexes all followed the general pattern of the Old Kingdom, and there was a return to the custom of surrounding the king's pyramid with the tombs of his favoured courtiers and nobles. But this period of peace and prosperity was not to last. The last rulers of the dynasty – Amenemmes IV and Sobeknefru – ushered in a period when the country sank yet again into a state of decline and the character of the ruler was insufficiently strong to remedy the evils that beset the land. Egypt's problems made it possible for foreigners to infiltrate the borders, and, on this occasion, to take possession of the country.

Let us first return, however, to the general religious trends apparent in the First Intermediate period and the Middle Kingdom, to see how the cult of the sun was gradually replaced by the widespread worship of Osiris, with the result that the non-royal tomb reached an unparalleled level of importance. Whenever possible, a non-royal person now attempted to provide himself with the best and safest tomb and the finest funerary goods he could afford. Never had the 'House of the Ka' been treated with such importance and reverence as during this period. Even the poor, unable to provide and equip elaborate tombs for their eternity, could now cling to some hope of immortality. As the means of attaining eternity became democratized, so the cult of the god Osiris developed and flourished. Unlike the exclusive cult of Re, which was so closely associated with the kingship that when the king fell, the cult became largely discredited, the cult of Osiris came to influence the whole of society.

However, during the Old Kingdom, the king had been identified with both Osiris and Re; the solar and Osirian cults were originally devised for the king alone, and there is no evidence of any direct conflict between them. At first, only the king was believed to become Osiris upon death, and all references to Osiris in the Pyramid Texts were associated with the king's own resurrection. From the Fifth dynasty onwards, the cult of Osiris flourished, despite the great power of the priesthood of Re, and gradually Osiris gained ascendancy as the royal god of the dead. The basic difference between the cults was that Re was primarily a god of the living, whereas Osiris was supreme deity in the underworld, but both deities symbolized, in different ways, the divine

ability to defeat death. The sun rose anew every morning, overcoming the death of the previous night, and every year Osiris was
resurrected from death, symbolized in the renewal of the vegetation. Both gods gave the Egyptians a hope of eternity and provided a pattern of death and re-birth. There is no evidence to
suggest a common origin between the solar and Osirian concepts,
but the basic similarity of function and their royal associations
linked the two gods in many important aspects of doctrine and
cult practice. It is impossible to trace the stages by which the
Osirian cult developed democratic features, but the ascendancy of
Osiris over Re is demonstrated in the funerary texts and monuments of the Middle Kingdom. The solar theories may have
continued to dominate the scene during the period of Heracleopolitan rule (the Ninth and Tenth dynasties), but the rise of
Osiris under the subsequent rule of their Theban rivals may have
been partly due to a political move to promote a deity who was not
so closely associated with the earlier rulers. Gradually, the great
provincial nobles adopted the funerary rites and rituals formerly
available only to the king, in the expectation of joining the gods
after death. Finally, the magical spells and formulae became generally available and even the poor could look forward to an individual eternity.

Although the kings of the Twelfth dynasty restored centralized
government, and once again strenghtened the chasm between
themselves and their subjects, they were always aware of their
non-royal origins. The dynasty depended upon acceptance at first
by the great nobles and later by the new middle-class. Although
the court moved back to the north, and the kings resumed the
building of pyramids, this renewal of Old Kingdom customs was
probably a superficial expression of the new royal power rather
than a return to earlier religious beliefs. The kings do not appear to
have made any attempt to restore the former status of the royal
sun-god, and, indeed, in addition to the cult of Osiris which
continued to flourish throughout the Middle Kingdom, the kings
of the Twelfth dynasty chose to elevate a new god to prominence
as royal deity. Amenemmes I and his successors were devoted to
their local Theban deity, Amun. It was during this period that the
temple of Amun was established at Karnak which was later to
become such an important force in Egypt.

We have already referred to the supposed early origin of the cult
of Osiris and to the associated mythology which may reflect

historical conditions either in the Predynastic period or in early dynastic times. However, the available sources throw little light on the historical origin of the god. Osiris was regarded as a god of vegetation; this may have been his primary role and he also played the part of life-giver and of the source of fertility in Egyptian mythology. Indeed, he personified the yearly re-birth of vegetation which occurred after the Nile had flooded its banks. Through this agricultural role, Osiris was also regarded as a corn-god, his re-birth being symbolized by the growth of the corn. Another aspect of his nature was expressed in his role as a moon-god.

It was probably from his personification of the re-birth of vegetation that he gained the qualities of a divine king and judge of the underworld. He came to be regarded as a symbol of victory over evil and his annual death and resurrection as a vegetation deity was interpreted in the wider sense as a victory of the power of life over death. In this role, he was installed not as a resurrected living king but as the king of the dead and of the underworld. He could thus promise continuation of life after death to his followers and also a successful trial before the divine judges. From this belief in Osiris as a dead, deified king developed the idea that every Egyptian pharaoh became an Osiris on death, and was succeeded by his heir – the living king who was Horus, the son and avenger of Osiris in the myth. Unlike the other deities Osiris concerned himself only with the affairs of the underworld. The importance of his cult and its associated beliefs were expressed not only in the funerary cult, but also in the concept of divine kingship and the related rituals, performed in the temples and at the king's accession and coronation.

According to classical sources, Osiris was also identified as a human king who had actually lived in Egypt. He had died at the hand of his enemy Seth and was later resurrected as a dead, deified ruler. He is always shown wearing a long white cloak, the crown of Upper Egypt, and carrying the insignia of a ruler. He is said to have originally brought agriculture and civilization to the Egyptians.

The origin of his name – 'Wsir' in hieroglyphs – is also obscure, and throws little light on his early history, although it has been tentatively translated as 'Mighty One' from the word wsr. Much has also been written regarding the relationship between Osiris and other Near Eastern deities, especially the gods Tammuz, Adonis and Dionysus. Stories associated with these deities show certain similarities, such as their identification as shepherd-gods, and the role played by a goddess who searches for the dead god and then bewails him and buries him. These deities also have a common feature in that they are represented as dead gods, linked with the growth of nature. However, there are also differences between them.

Three main sources refer to this myth and the rituals associated with Osiris. We have already mentioned the oldest source – the Pyramid Texts – which provide the earliest information. There are also the inscriptions and reliefs on the walls of some of the temples, especially those dating from the Graeco-Roman period. These record the rites which accompanied the annual festivals held in honour of the god at centres throughout Egypt. Finally, the earliest complete version of the Myth of Osiris is preserved in the writings of Plutarch, which date to the later period of Egyptian history. This version is a predominantly Greek rendering of the myth and it may not be an accurate reflection of the earlier tradition. Many references to Osiris of course exist in the Egyptian texts, but no complete Egyptian account has ever been found, possibly because the myth was known only through word of mouth in the earlier period.

However obscure the origins of Osiris appear today, his influence grew and extended throughout the Old Kingdom so that his cult eventually rivalled the solar cult itself. The troubles of the First Intermediate period and the subsequent rise of the Middle Kingdom provided the ideal conditions in which Osiris could replace the fallen image of the king as a symbol of strength, and could offer help to ordinary people. By the Middle Kingdom he could even promise them a chance of a life after death. There is some controversy over the site of Osiris' first cult-centre in Egypt. He had close connections both with Busiris in the Delta and with Abydos in Upper Egypt. However, by the Middle Kingdom, his centre was firmly established at Abydos. People came on pilgrimages, or made arrangements to be buried there, or set up stelae, or had their mummies transported to Abydos before being returned for burial in their local cemeteries. Abydos was believed to be the actual site of the burial of Osiris, and any direct contact with the place was thought to increase the individual's chance of joining in the god's resurrection.

Abydos had long associations with royal burials and the accompanying rituals, for the kings of the early dynasties built funerary places here, although it is uncertain whether these were tombs or merely cenotaphs. Interest in Abydos as a major religious centre and place of pilgrimage was renewed in the Middle Kingdom. It replaced Heliopolis, centre of the sun-god, as the focal point for royal pilgrimages. Such a move was perhaps politically motivated and encouraged by the rulers of the period who wished to dis-associate themselves from the religious preferences of the Old Kingdom kings. Thus, Abydos became a place of burial for those who could afford it, and a place of pilgrimage for others. Even those unable to make the pilgrimage in life were provided with another opportunity to take part in the god's festival. From the end of the Old Kingdom onwards, model boats, complete with oars and sailors, were placed in the tombs to enable the tomb-owner to journey by river to the great Abydos festival.

Something of the excitement and mystery of this festival can be gleaned from a contemporary record – the stela of a man named Ikhernofret – who was a chief treasurer in the reign of King Sesostris III. He was sent to Abydos to reorganize the cult of Osiris and to replenish the temple furnishings. Ikhernofret describes how he took part in the Mystery Plays which were held annually at Abydos from the Twelfth dynasty onwards. The plays were performed by the priests and celebrated events in the life and death of Osiris. Some sequences were staged outside the temple precinct and watched by the pilgrims, who were known as the 'Followers of Thoth'. The most sacred rites were enacted inside the temple, probably in special chambers devoted to this annual event. They sought to ensure the resurrection of the god and his followers and also to benefit the deceased king who had become an Osiris. The festival was held in the last month of the inundation of the Nile, and was a time of great rejoicing not only for the priests but also for the large crowds who had travelled many miles to witness this colourful annual 'miracle'. These rites dramatized the 'death' of the vegetation through scarcity of water, and the final return of new growth when the waters subsided, in addition to the death and re-birth of the god Osiris. In their performance the priests hoped to exert their influence over natural events, to ensure a good harvest, to commemorate the resurrection of Osiris, and to celebrate the accession of the king to the throne – as Horus, the son and heir of Osiris.

Despite this wonderful annual spectacle with its mass appeal, it was in his promise of eternity to all his followers, and not just to the king, that Osiris' great attraction lay. We have already seen that the Egyptian had various concepts of the afterlife, and that these were to some extent interchangeable. Only the king had originally had access to the solar afterlife and an eternity spent in the tomb presupposed the status and wealth necessary to provide and equip a tomb sufficiently. However, subject to certain conditions of entry, the Osirian afterlife had no such limitations. It was thought of as a place of lush vegetation, where continuous springtime delighted the inhabitants and where the harvests never failed. It was known as the 'Fields of Reeds', and those whose earthly conduct had enabled them to achieve eternity passed their days here in cultivation of the abundant crops. According to some this world lay below the western horizon, or, according to others, on a group of islands only reached by boat. Osiris reigned here as king and judge of the dead. His realm resembled the conditions known in the world of the living, but those lucky enough to reach his land were untroubled by the trials and tribulations of earthly existence.

However, entry was dependent on the fulfilment of certain conditions. First, the correct burial procedure had to be observed and the deceased supplied with a continuing store of food and drink. More important still was the day of divine judgment which each man or woman had to face. Osiris himself had been tried before a tribunal of divine judges; he had been defended by Thoth and found innocent of all evil. The gods thereupon declared him 'True of Voice', and granted him immortality. This immortality now became a feature of funerary beliefs in relation to ordinary people. Everyone who could establish his worthiness before a tribunal of forty-two divine judges, various other deities, and Osiris, became eligible for immortality. A man affirmed the purity of his soul by reciting the 'Negative Confession', and thus stressing his morality. During the trial, the deceased addressed each of his judges by name; he then declared his innocence of any serious crimes or misdemeanours during his life on earth. Sometimes, knowledge of magic or spells could deceive the gods at this stage of the trial, but the second part of the ordeal involved further examination, and this event is depicted in many funerary scenes. The dead person was accompanied by the deities Thoth, Ma'at and Anubis, and the scene was dominated by a large pair of scales. The attendant goddesses of fate and destiny testified concerning the dead man's character and Thoth, god of writing, wisdom and literature, recorded the verdict. Anubis, god of embalming, then placed the heart of the deceased into one of the pans of the scales (the heart being regarded as the seat of the intellect and the emotions), and this was balanced in the other pan by a feather, the symbol of truth and justice. The deceased anxiously awaited the result of the investigation; his soul, depicted as a human-headed bird, was shown separately. If the deceased was not guilty the heart and the feather would balance each other. The verdict was then recorded by Thoth and the man was declared free from sin. After the tribunal of gods had accepted the verdict, the man would be re-united with his soul, and they would pass eternity together in the Osirian underworld. The guilty man, however, faced a terrible fate; he would be thrown to a beast, part-feline, part-hippopotamus and part-crocodile, which crouched near the scales, waiting to devour the hearts of the guilty. From the Eleventh dynasty onwards, it became the regular custom to attach the word 'justified' to the name of every deceased Egyptian, thus indicating their success in the trial before the divine judges, and their moral fitness to be granted immortality. Another naming procedure became widespread during the Middle Kingdom; the name of Osiris was inserted as a title before the name of the deceased. Originally this custom had been based on the theory that every king became an Osiris upon death; it was then extended to members of the royal family, to the nobility, and finally to all Egyptians who had attained immortality. In due course, both these titles simply came to have the meaning of 'deceased' when they were attached to a person's name, and lost their original connotations. Although magic and suitable spells were considered methods of assisting a man's passage into the next world, access to the realm of Osiris was primarily granted on evidence of good character. The development of the cult of Osiris and the democratization of the afterlife had profound effects upon funerary customs and we can now examine the tombs and tomb equipment of this period.

We know that the tombs of the nomarchs of the First Intermediate period, and, to a lesser extent, during the Middle Kingdom, were built near the capital city of each local ruler. Rock-cut tombs were prepared in the nearby cliffs around which courtiers were buried in similar tombs. Each was designed to a general plan, which incorporated a portico with two or more columns, or a terraced courtyard. From this, a great door led into a columned hall, where the columns were cut out of the rock. This gave access to a small room or niche which contained the owner's statue and here offerings would have been placed in front of the statue. In order to deter tomb-robbers, the burial chamber was situated beyond the chapel containing the statue, and was sometimes entered through a section in the floor of the hall. One of the most remarkable features of these tombs was the fact that they were cut out of the cliff face itself, but the painted scenes which decorated the hall also provide fascinating insight into the art and level of craftsmanship of this period. The art-forms had become 'localized' after the decentralization of the country at the end of the Old Kingdom; large building projects were no longer being carried out for the king, and a flourishing industry grew to meet the needs of the provincial nobility. Local artisans were employed to decorate these tombs and to produce non-royal tomb statuary, and, although the old forms continued, debased, in some areas, the craftsmen were little influenced by the classical style of the Memphite school which had prospered during the Old Kingdom. Gradually although the content of the tomb scenes remained the same, the execution of the reliefs and paintings became much cruder and, despite the great feudal districts' patronage of their own local schools of craftsmen, and the natural local variation and interpretation, the new source of inspiration for all funerary art of this period was to be Thebes. From the new southern capital a style developed which was crude, but realistic and vigorous. Its main characteristics were a combination of relief, detail, and the use of new proportions in the representation of the human figure, now shown with a small head, a tall, slender body and an exaggerated distance between the waist and the feet.

The return of centralized power in the Twelfth dynasty, the renewed demand for royal statuary, the return to pyramid-building, and the partial revival of Old Kingdom styles did not obliterate the Theban influence. Although Memphite influence returned to royal and non-royal art, the dynamic qualities of the Theban style which sprang up during the Eleventh dynasty are still present in the new forms. In general, although some differences do exist between the style and execution of the wall scenes in the tombs of the First Intermediate period and those of the Middle Kingdom, the funerary equipment placed in these tombs was very similar in both periods.

With the gradual increase in demand for funerary goods for non-royal Egyptians, certain features of the funerary paraphenalia underwent change and development. The use of canopic jars –

stone or pottery vessels which contained the mummified viscera of the deceased – became more widespread. The four jars in each set were placed in a wooden chest which was a smaller version of the brightly-painted rectangular coffins which became popular at this time. The canopic chest was usually placed in a square niche cut into the wall of the burial chamber.

Those who could afford the expense provided lavish and varied equipment for the burial chamber. During the First Intermediate period, the cartonnage mask, which was placed over the face of the mummy, and which had originated in the Old Kingdom, became more lifelike. Usually the facial features were stylized and bore no direct resemblance to the owner, but now they were carefully painted and the mask served as a substitute for the deceased in the event of his mummy suffering damage. It was from these masks that the anthropoid or body coffins of the Twelfth dynasty probably developed. These coffins were at first made of cartonnage, but were later constructed of wood. They were mummiform in shape and design, and the funerary trappings found on the body within the coffin – such as the broad collar, the girdle, bandaging and other decorations – were also painted on the outside of the coffin. Since the deceased was now identified with Osiris after death, these coffins represented him as an Osiris; thus, the symbols of divinity and kingship, such as a false beard and a uraeus on the forehead, were added, in wood, to the mummiform coffin. The body coffin was rendered even more lifelike by inserting inlaid eyes of obsidian and alabaster. These colourful, often beautifully painted coffins would have been selected by the prospective owner or his relatives from a large stock of funerary equipment available to all who could afford such items. The wealthy man would also have supplied himself with a rectangular outer coffin, which was usually made of wood, although royalty and the great nobles were sometimes provided with stone coffins. The most common type of wooden coffin had a flat or vaulted lid and was widely used by all classes of people until the end of the Middle Kingdom. At first these were decorated with horizontal lines of inscription, but many also display distinctive and brightly painted geometric designs. A pair of eyes was painted on the east or left side of the coffin, to enable the deceased to 'look out' towards the food offerings which would be brought to the tomb by his relatives. Food offerings were also sometimes painted on the coffin itself.

The inscriptions are a perfect example of the custom of this period of a royal practice being handed down to all who could afford it. Earlier kings had used magic spells to assist them in overcoming obstacles which faced them in the tomb and beyond. We have seen that these spells, known as the Pyramid Texts, were written up in their pyramids. Now, in the First Intermediate period, these texts were purloined by the local rulers, and eventually, during the Middle Kingdom, this corpus of funerary magic became available to all those who could afford such elaborate preparations. In an abbreviated, modified form, these texts were written on the coffins of the dead and today they are known as the 'Coffin Texts'. The spells still consisted of direct and affirmative statements which were beneficial to the deceased and which constantly denied death and supported eternal life. The repetitive phrases were believed to bring about the desired result, and the spells sought to cover every adverse situation which the deceased might encounter when journeying along that dangerous path from this world to the next. The texts were adapted, of course, for commoners, some additions were introduced to meet the requirements of the new clients, and cursive hieroglyphic script was used to write the texts on the coffins. The Coffin Texts only occurred during this period, although there was a brief revival during the Twenty-sixth dynasty, and a more immediate development of these texts took place during the New Kingdom, when they were written on papyrus, and became known, in this modified form, as the *Book of the Dead*.

Other funerary equipment became important and this included greater use of servant figurines. Although these were placed in the tombs of the nobles in the Fifth dynasty, they became an increasingly important feature in the 'House of the Ka', and in the First Intermediate period, the number and variety of models performing different tasks and functions on behalf of the tomb-owner developed considerably. The original named statue of the tomb-owner, accompanied by models of members of his family and of a few servants now became only one aspect of this type of equipment. Servant models, often arranged in groups pursuing some activity related to food-production or preparation, were included in many tombs and could be 'brought to life' to carry out their master's will. In addition to models of women grinding corn, men at work ploughing, fishing, brewing, making bread, and slaughtering animals (activities which had all been painted in the wall

scenes in Old Kingdom tombs), there were now models representing the fine house, estate, and herds of the tomb owner. Weavers
provided clothing and troops of soldiers ensured the safety of their
master in a period of general unrest and discontent. Model boats
may have been intended to enable the deceased to make the
pilgrimage by river to the sacred city of Abydos, or to sail in the
west – the realm of the dead. Ordinary people might supply
themselves with one or two boats, but the nobles were often
accompanied by models of complete fleets, including different
craft for different requirements. The boats were finely made,
carved of wood, and were equipped with sails, rudder, oars,
deck-cabin, and crew. Personal entertainment of the deceased was
not ignored. Models of concubine figures with inlaid eyes and
locks of real hair have been found together with harpists who
entertained at the banquets, and dwarfs who acted as attendants
and entertainers at the great houses. This strange, miniature world
of the tomb models reflects the lifestyle on the great estates of the
period and provides the Egyptologist with a wealth of information.

Perhaps most curious, however, is one special group of funerary
models which was introduced in the First Intermediate period.
Today, these are called *ushabti* figures and must be known to any
visitor to a museum with an Egyptian collection. They were made
of durable material and produced in large numbers. Although the
origin of the word *ushabti* is uncertain, the use for which these
figures were intended is closely linked with the increasingly
important cult of Osiris. The afterlife which Osiris promised his
followers involved, as we have seen, compulsory agricultural
labours in the fields of Osiris. At first the wealthy, but eventually
others also, began to provide themselves with substitute workers
in the form of these figurines who would undertake these undesirable duties on their behalf, leaving them free to pursue activities
more to their liking. The original figurines had their own small
coffins but were later replaced by mummiform statuettes of
wood, stone or faience; these were usually enscribed with the
name of the owner and the special magical formula which would
enable the dead man to call the *ushabti* to his service. In their later,
fully developed form, agricultural tools, such as a mattock, hoe
and seed box, were painted or carved on many of the figurines.
Hundreds of *ushabti* figures would be included in one tomb – it is
sometimes claimed that they numbered one for each day of the

year, – and overseer figurines, each with a stiffened, flared skirt and a whip, would also be present, to supervise the workforce of *ushabti* figures. Gradually, by the New Kingdom, these figurines came to replace the wooden models of servants of the Old and Middle Kingdom tombs. Faience became the most widespread material used for *ushabtis*. Indeed, the *ushabti* figures can be dated from their material, style, decoration and inscription. Even the size and quality of the figure gives an indication of the date of the piece, for these reflect the contemporary strength and prosperity of Egypt. From the Twenty-first dynasty onwards, the small, undecorated *ushabti* is common and mass production in clay moulds lowered the general quality, whereas during the Eighteenth and Twenty-sixth dynasties (when Egypt experienced a brief revival of excellence in funerary and religious arts), the *ushabti* figures were finely produced. These figurines were one of the most durable forms of funerary art, and perhaps more than any others were most closely identified with the Osirian afterlife.

Other examples of funerary equipment during this period included the use of food offering trays which had the same function as those of the earlier dynasties, and the introduction of 'soul-houses' – model pottery houses with open courtyards at the front. The goods which the owner placed in his tomb, whether they were clothes, toilet equipment, cosmetics, toys and games, or the exquisite jewellery of the period, showed the attention now lavished on the tomb of a non-royal person.

During the First Intermediate period and the Middle Kingdom, the 'House of the Ka' and its contents came to have great importance for an increasing number of people, and although the later kings to some extent revived their ancient power and glory, the distance which the rulers of the Old Kingdom had placed between themselves and their subjects in death was never again so apparent.

# 7 *King of Gods*

The brilliant period which saw the rise to fame of the god Osiris came to an end with the reign of Queen Sobkneferu, the last ruler of the Twelfth dynasty. The writer Manetho states that the Thirteenth dynasty consisted of 'sixty kings of Diospolis' (Thebes) 'who reigned for 453 years'. This figure is erroneous and should read '153 years', but the Thirteenth dynasty certainly appears to have been a time of rapid succession of rulers. These probably reigned as subordinates to a line of powerful and dominating viziers, but nevertheless, central government continued and was apparently respected inside Egypt and elsewhere for over a hundred years.

However, at least one district enjoyed separate government during the Thirteenth dynasty and for a period of about thirty years after its downfall. Described as the Fourteenth dynasty in Manetho's list, it consisted of a long line of local rulers who reigned independently in the district of Xois; they had seceded from the rest of the country at the end of the Twelfth dynasty in 1786 BC, and thereafter pursued their own course.

The Thirteenth dynasty came to an end when foreigners entered Egypt and took over the rule of the country. These people have become known as the 'Hyksos', and their origin and organization have been the subject of much discussion. It was originally thought that they were members of a single Asiatic nation or group who had an empire already established in Palestine and even beyond, and that they came to Egypt with their army, as a horde invasion. They might have included Indo-Aryan elements from the north, such as the people referred to as 'Hurrians'. These theories have more recently been modified. It seems more likely that small groups infiltrated into the Delta during the period of weak government throughout the Thirteenth dynasty, and that they were made up of different western Asiatic groups although their names indicate that many were of a Semitic origin. The name 'Hyksos' which is given to them by Manetho, and which has been erroneously translated as 'Shepherd Kings', is in fact derived from the Egyptian words meaning 'Rulers of foreign lands'. This term was earlier applied to the petty chieftains of the Beduin and local tribes who had persistently threatened Egypt's northern borders. It is now considered that these people were probably Egypt's old enemies, perhaps forced to find new homes because of disturbances and pressures in parts of Asia Minor. They saw the opportunity which weak rulership in Egypt offered and seized the chance to infiltrate and settle inside Egypt.

Manetho records that the Hyksos subdued Egypt in the reign of a King 'Tutimaios' who has been tentatively identified as King Dudimose. He recounts that Memphis, the capital city, was taken and occupied by the Hyksos ruler Salitis. This occurred in 1674 BC, and from then onwards, the native rulers of the Thirteenth dynasty became merely local dynasts. Power passed to the Hyksos, and they are grouped by Manetho into the contemporaneous Fifteenth and Sixteenth dynasties. A new centre of native semi-independence was established at Thebes from about 1650 BC onwards; the princes who ruled here, albeit under the control of the Hyksos in the north, formed the Seventeenth dynasty and it was they who eventually drove the Hyksos from Egypt and founded the New Kingdom.

However, the foreigners ruled Egypt for many years and profoundly changed the outlook of the native inhabitants. It is difficult to assess the quality of their rule, since most of the surviving information about them is from later Egyptian propagandist sources. The later writer Josephus cites a section of Manetho's history in his own work, and relates that the Hyksos gained Egypt without a struggle and then proceeded to burn the cities and the temples of the gods. Such statements seem contradictory, because it is more plausible that such destruction came about as the result of native resistance to the conquerors. We are told that the Hyksos proceeded to elect one of themselves as King; he was named Salitis, and, having established his capital at Memphis, he rebuilt a city in the Delta and garrisoned it with 240,000 men. He is portrayed as a tough and avaricious ruler who imposed heavy taxes on the Egyptians.

The Hyksos' reaction to their new home and conquered subjects does not indicate that they brought with them a highly developed or organized civilization of their own to impose on Egypt. In fact, the contrary is true, for they appear to have adopted Egyptian customs and to have employed native personnel to assist them in running the country. It is only towards the end of their occupation, when they faced local insurrection, that they introduced superior military weapons and techniques from outside to try to uphold their power against the Egyptians. Indeed, they were not a convincing cohesive ethnic group although they probably had a general similarity of custom and culture. The period of Hyksos' rule is now regarded as a change of rulers rather than as a mass invasion.

The Hyksos have been depicted as barbarous and ruthless overlords by the Egyptian propagandists of the New Kingdom onwards, but there is little evidence to support such a view. The native people certainly would have been taxed, and, as rulers, they would have taken tribute from the vassal regions in the south, but there was no break in the tradtion of using the existing Egyptian administrative system and officials. With little of their own culture to introduce, the Hyksos rulers supported native arts and crafts and borrowed from them. Temple building and the production of works of art continued, and literary composition in the Egyptian style still flourished. These rulers adopted the traditional titles of the kings of Egypt and wrote their names in hieroglyphs. Perhaps the most distinctive contribution of this period in terms of the minor arts was the production of large numbers of stone scarabs decorated with scroll designs.

Other dynasties had sought the protection of a major deity and the Hyksos followed this pattern, choosing Seth as their special royal god. His centre of worship was at Avaris, the capital which they had established. He was probably not so much the god of the old Horus and Seth conflict but possessed characteristics which were similar to one of their own Asiatic deities. He was not in any way an exclusive god, however, and other Egyptian gods were honoured by the Hyksos. They regarded Re, the sun-god, as their protector, even though his associations with earlier native rulers were so long-standing, and they incorporated his name in some of their royal titles so that, perhaps surprisingly, we see amongst the Hyksos rulers such names as Mayebre Sheshi, Seuserenre Khyan, Auserre Apophis I, Khauserre and Sekhaenre.

Nevertheless for reasons which are not entirely clear, this period of foreign rule came to be regarded by later generations as a time of disaster for the country and its people. Perhaps the simple fact that the kings were not Egyptian was sufficiently irksome to the people to create the hatred which was later expressed against the Hyksos, and to promote the reverence which was shown to the princes of the Seventeenth dynasty who freed the country from this burden.

The Hyksos occupation certainly brought new blood and new ideas; it changed the political and mental character of the Egyptians and prepared them for the role which they were soon to play as empire-builders. Until then, Egypt had not played a part in the general development in Asia Minor, although strong trading links had existed from early times. The Egyptians, requiring access to the source of the gold and hard stone, had colonized Nubia over a period of many years, but the lands of their northerly neighbours had never exerted the same attraction in terms of raw materials. Since they were essentially a non-aggressive people who were well satisfied with their own country and its resources, the Egyptians had never attempted to expand in this direction and to impose their rule on other peoples. The infiltration of the Hyksos and the subsequent period of foreign domination rudely awakened them from their complacency. With their new techniques and weapons and their close contacts with Asia Minor, the Hyksos brought a new dimension to Egyptian thought and forced upon them the unpleasant awareness that other people did exist beyond Egypt's boundaries who could enter and conquer Egypt. Only by becoming aggressive and expanding into the countries of Asia Minor could Egypt now protect her own boundaries and prevent a repetition of this foreign domination.

Apart from the psychological aspect, the Hyksos gave the Egyptians knowledge of the war techniques which helped the rulers of the Eighteenth dynasty to win their empire. Advanced metal skills, including the use of the bellows, the composite bow, the khepesh-sword, and improved bronze daggers were some of the innovations introduced in the Hyksos period. Although the horse and the horse-drawn chariot may have been known before this period, the earliest textual reference to their use in Egypt for warfare dates to the end of the Hyksos period. There were also domestic innovations such as the lute and the lyre, and the vertical loom, and humped cattle were apparently introduced at this time.

In the New Kingdom, a professional army was now set up which consisted of paid soldiers; many received land as a gift from the king and this remained in the family for as long as the family fought for Egypt. In both organization and attitude, the new army was a great improvement on earlier forces which had been formed locally and generally consisted of conscripted men.

The exact course of events which led to direct conflict between the Egyptians and their Hyksos overlords is unknown, but the spearhead of native dissidents was provided by the line of brilliant princes who ruled at Thebes as vassals of the Hyksos. The conflict developed in the reign of the Hyksos ruler Apophis who was driven north as far as the Fayoum by the southerners, led by the Thebans. His successors enjoyed only a brief period of rule before Avaris, the capital, fell and the hated overlords were eventually driven from Egypt in about 1567 BC. Later generations of Egyptians glorified the Thebans Seqenenre II, Kamose and Amosis I (who became the first ruler of the Eighteenth dynasty) as the heroes who had expelled the Hyksos. The Egyptians eventually pursued them into southern Palestine where the remnants of their power were finally destroyed.

The early rulers of the Eighteenth dynasty gave due credit to their immediate ancestors for their own brilliant rise to fame as founders of Egypt's Empire. The local Theban dynasts were undoubtedly able and ambitious men who, in local isolation, had attempted to carry on the traditions of the Middle Kingdom throughout the Hyksos interlude. These local rulers of the Seventeenth dynasty built small mud-brick pyramids for themselves at Dira Abu'n-Naga in western Thebes; they produced traditional funerary and other goods using local craftsmen and materials, and they preserved earlier knowledge in their writings. A man named Nubkheperre Inyotef appears to have been regarded as the first important ruler of this line and his wife, Sobkemsaf, was honoured as an ancestress of the Eighteenth dynasty. Other much revered rulers were Seqenenre Tao I and his wife, Tetisheri, and their children Seqenenre Tao II and Ahhotpe who were both brother and sister and husband and wife. The mummy of Seqenenre Tao II shows evidence of severe head wounds and it is probable that these may have resulted from his battle against the Hyksos and that they were the cause of his death. His son, Kamose, continued the fight. Not only were these brave warrior kings held in high esteem by later generations, but their wives were also accorded considerable honour as co-founders of the New Kingdom.

However, greatest praise and glory were also given to the god who had supported their independence and had assisted them to gain ascendancy over the foreigners. This was Amun, the deity worshipped by the Thebans since the beginning of the Twelfth dynasty. Originally one of the deities of the Hermopolitan *ogdoad*, Amun was probably a god of the air, whose name may have meant 'The Hidden One'. He came to have associations with Min, the ithyphallic god whose main centres were at Koptos and Akhmim, and both gods took a human form. They each wore a headdress with two tall plumes, carried the flail, and Amun, as well as Min, is sometimes represented in ithyphallic form. At some time in the First Intermediate period, Amun was apparently brought to Thebes, and as the god of the victorious Theban rulers, in the Twelfth dynasty he became the great state god, replacing Montu, the war-god worshipped by the kings of the Eleventh dynasty. Throughout the Middle Kingdom, Amun's power increased and during the subsequent Hyksos domination, the Thebans continued to worship him with unabated loyalty. During the Seventeenth dynasty, the temple of Min (a god regarded as a variant form of Amun) at Koptos was restored, and the Theban ruler Seqenenre, according to a famous papyrus, did not worship 'any god which is in (the entire land) except Amen-Re, King of the gods'.

Their loyalty to Amun was rewarded by supreme power in Egypt, and the Thebans in turn elevated the god to a position of unprecedented importance. Not only did they regard him as responsible for their victory against the Hyksos but also as the reason for their considerable military successes against their enemies in Asia Minor.

However, the god's absolute supremacy was not assured until the old sun-god had been effectively co-ordinated with Amun. To prevent rivalry between the two deities, the Thebans created the all-powerful god Amen-Re; thus, Amun absorbed all the qualities and features of the older god, and especially his characteristics as the protector and supporter of royalty. The priests of Re at Heliopolis cannot have been kindly disposed to this southern usurping of their deity but such was the power of Amen-Re and the magnitude of his priesthood that it is unlikely that any other cult could offer realistic opposition. In fact, it was the solar elements which eventually dominated the character of the new deity; he wore the important symbols of the old sun-god and retained his characteristics and mythology at the expense of the earlier local form of Amun. As we have already seen, it was the solar nature of Amen-Re which was stressed in the New Kingdom hymns to the god.

By the middle of the Eighteenth dynasty, the Egyptian empire was well established in Asia Minor, and after the reign of Amenophis II, the role of Amen-Re underwent a subtle change. More emphasis was placed on his function as a creator of mankind and a ruler of both the Egyptians and their subjects. To promote this aspect of their god, it was essential that the priesthood of Amen-Re should establish the claim of Thebes, his cult-centre, to be the place of creation. In order to do this, all earlier important cosmogonies had to be ousted by the Theban creation myth.

A Theban cosmogony was now promoted which incorporated earlier myths but which was based on the primary role of Amun as the creator-god, and the importance of the site of Thebes, where the primordial mound was said to have first risen out of the waters of Nun; here Amun had created mankind, and the city of Thebes was regarded as the model for all later centres. The very nature of Amun – as a god of the air – fitted easily into the new concept of the invisible but all powerful creator-god. The cycle commenced when Amun created himself in secret and came out of an egg on the primeval mound. All other forms and aspects of earlier creator gods – such as the *ogdoad* of Hermopolis, Tatenen who personified the primeval mound at Memphis, and Re of Heliopolis – were now combined within Amun. He was the means of creating all the other systems and gods.

In his mythology he was 'king of the gods' and ruled all other deities, but also, since they were all only variant aspects of Amun, he could take on any of their forms or powers at will. These included his solar characteristics from Re, his identification with the moon, and his close associations with Min, the fertility god, and Ptah, the creator-god of Memphis. Another aspect of his powers of fertility involved the ram; he was believed to be present in the ram and the concept is magnificently captured in the triumphal avenue of ram-headed sphinxes which mark the main approach to his great temple at Karnak. In yet another form, he was represented as a goose and called the 'Great Cackler'.

In his original form in the Heliopolitan *ogoad*, Amun was

provided with a consort whose name – Amaunet – is derived from
his own. However, when his cult became established at Karnak, he
formed a divine triad there with a wife – Mut, the vulture goddess,
and their son – Khonsu, the falcon-headed moon god.

Amen-Re became chiefly the royal god, the protector of the
kings whose line he had placed on the throne of Egypt. The king,
previously the 'son of Re', was now the son of 'his father Amun',
and on this unique relationship rested his right to claim the throne
of Egypt. The former royal burial places in the north and at the
great religious centre of Abydos were now abandoned and the
kings elected to be buried in western Thebes, near to Amen-Re's
cult-centre. Here, the political and religious power of the country
converged. Thebes reigned supreme as the site of the capital city,
the cult-centre of the great state god and the royal necropolis.

The royal burial sites of the New Kingdom lay on the west bank
of the river, opposite the thriving city of Thebes which was
dominated by the magnificent temples of Karnak and Luxor.
Beyond the flat cultivated plain on the west bank, there are the
awe-inspiring, bleak and barren Theban hills; the natural shape
and colouring of which are reminiscent of the pyramid form and
this may have been one reason why the kings now chose to be
buried here. The Egyptians referred to this mass as 'the Peak' and
regarded it as the protector of the dead resting in the desolate
valleys below. Here, in a barren, rocky, narrow valley, known
today as the Valley of the Kings, the rulers, from Amenophis I of
the Eighteenth dynasty onwards, were buried in deep rock-cut
tombs. These often cut deeply into the side of the mountain and
were designed to defy the tomb-robbers, but to no avail. In a
nearby valley lay the bodies of the favourite royal wives and some
of the princes, in tombs only slightly less elaborate than those of
the kings. Favoured courtiers and other important and wealthy
nobles were also buried in the vicinity. The very isolation and
inaccessibility of these areas must have prompted the kings to
select such a burial place, which, unlike the earlier pyramids,
would not be immediately apparent to tomb-robbers. However,
all the known royal tombs, except the famed one belonging to the
boy-king Tutankhamun, which escaped with only minor plundering, were entered and robbed in antiquity. The royal mummies
were stripped of their jewellery and the contents of the tombs
removed. Later, the priests of the Twenty-first dynasty rescued
the mummies and buried them again in two caches, so that the

bodies of the deceased would be preserved intact for the benefit of the afterlife.

Nevertheless despite the destruction wrought by the robbers, the tombs remain, with their superbly decorated chambers. One can only marvel at the succession of rooms and corridors in the royal tombs, hewn from the rock, and decorated with scenes representing the royal combat against evil forces. These were taken from the sacred books and were believed to assist the passage of the dead king into the next world. The tombs of the nobles, however, show delightful and informative aspects of everday life during this period, not only of the well-to-do tomb-owners but of their servants and workers. We see again the agricultural and domestic themes of earlier times, but the wider relationship with Egypt's foreign neighbours is now apparent. Envoys bring tribute and presents to Egypt from vassal states and countries who court Egypt's favours, and the general excitement and bustle of a great and powerful country with a large empire still pervades these scenes in the silent tombs at Thebes.

Below the rocky valleys with their inhospitable terrain, the wide cultivated plain stretches out to the Nile, and here the remains of the once magnificent mortuary temples of these kings are to be found. Formerly associated with the king's pyramid or tomb and an integral part of the burial complex, the limited building area in the Valley of the Kings now prevented the burial place being adjacent to its chapel or temple. From the New Kingdom onwards, mortuary temples were separated from the royal tomb, although their ritual function remained closely linked.

During this period, the myth that each king was the offspring of his human mother (the previous king's Great Royal Wife) by the chief god was perpetuated, and the king's chief wife was known as the 'God's Wife of Amun'. Amen-Re thus usurped Re as the divine father of the kings of Egypt, granting them the right to rule, and these royal women played an important part in the succession. They may even have participated in the god's temple cult, through a deputy.

Amen-Re had undoubtedly become a 'national god' who was both an empire builder and a great state deity. He was also a god whom the ordinary people worshipped. The kings and the priesthood of Amun succeeded in raising his status above that of all other deities, and in establishing Thebes not only as the main royal residence city and capital of the empire but also as the major religious centre. New temples and cult centres were built for Amen-Re in many parts of Egypt and here he often gained ascendancy over older local gods. Eventually, he became the supreme god of Egypt, and his priests claimed the right to have certain supervisory powers over the other priesthoods. They even took over the titles of the high priests of previously important gods such as Re and Ptah. The priesthood of Amen-Re at Karnak ultimately acquired such importance that it became a major political and economic factor in Egypt.

The key factor in their advancement was of course the continuing generosity of the king to the god. We have seen that the kings of the Eighteenth dynasty regarded their success in driving out the Hyksos and later in establishing their empire in Asia Minor as the work of Amen-Re. Throughout the early and middle parts of the Eighteenth dynasty, they strove to repay their debt to the god by donating lavishly to his cult. Early in the dynasty, Egypt expanded into an empire state; not only did the Theban kings restore Egypt's control over Nubia in the south, but the memory of the Hyksos occupation still clear, they now turned their attention to the many small states to the north and east. Expeditions set out, led by the kings, to subdue these small independent cities and states in Palestine, and to ensure their future allegiance to Egypt. Egypt was not the only great state to have an interest in the loyalty of these people, and Egyptian policy in Asia Minor led, at different periods, to confrontation with the two other nations who posed a threat to Egypt's dominance of the area. The Egyptians took up arms against both the Mitannians and the Hittites and major battles were fought with varying degrees of success for both sides. However, the Egyptians were able to establish the first empire, controlling an area which stretched from Nubia to the River Euphrates. Subsequently, larger and more centrally organized empires were established by the Assyrians and the Persians, but the Egyptian empire was a loose association; native governors were appointed to the cities and states who were loyal to Egypt and their political inclinations were further enforced by the removal to Egypt of their sons. Not only did they act as hostages for their fathers' good behaviour but the young men were educated in the Egyptian system and would eventually be returned to their homes as loyal vassal rulers of the Egyptians.

The campaigns in Asia Minor brought Egypt booty, and in addition to this, the vassal states paid tribute to Egypt. Already rich in her own natural resources, Egypt now enjoyed a period of unprecedented wealth and luxury. The kings did not forget their patron, and honoured Amen-Re as never before with vast endowments of property and personnel. New temples were built and old ones were repaired; large estates were established to support the temples and their staff. Other gods received some share of the spoil, but Amen-Re's endowments surpassed all others.

The temple of Amun at Karnak benefited directly from the foreign campaigns; raw materials, prisoners-of-war and slaves were presented to the temple to be used in the service of the god. The temple also owned mines where materials were excavated for the fine temple equipment which was produced in the temple workshops. It owned estates, often of the best land, where live-stock was reared, crops were grown and gardens and vineyards tended, to supply the temple needs. The temple provided work for large numbers of men and women who, apart from carrying out religious duties, were employed to administer the temple complex and its estates or to labour in various ways for the god. Other areas of the country also paid rent to the temple; this was paid in kind and was collected by the temple's fleet of ships and stored at Karnak in magazines. Unlike other tax-payers, the temples were protected by royal decrees from the extortions of the Crown agents, although some kind of tax appears to have been levied on them.

When one visits the complex of buildings known as the Temple of Amun at Karnak, it is apparent that this was once a great and powerful centre, at the heart of the political and economic life of Egypt as well as being a place of religious sanctity. At first sight, it is bewildering, with its confusion of courtyards, colonnades, obel-isks and pylons. The complex was started in the Twelfth dynasty, and the rulers of the New Kingdom and subsequent periods enlarged it and altered it many times. The buildings which can be seen today date mainly to the reigns of the kings of the Eighteenth and Nineteenth dynasties, especially Tuthmosis III, Amenophis III, Ramesses I, Sethos I, Ramesses II, Sethos II and Ramesses III; of the Twenty-second and Twenty-fifth dynasties, and of the Ptolemaic period. Constant alteration and expansion would have taken place, with each ruler attempting to surpass his predecessors in honouring the god. Smaller temples dedicated to other deities which had not been part of Amun's original complex were eventually absorbed into his cult-centre increasing his ever-growing power and influence.

The most important area of the whole complex is the Great Temple of Amun. Today, this is approached from the west and the visitor walks down an avenue of ram-headed sphinxes and through the first pylon into the Great Court, taking the same route which victorious pharaohs must have followed when they returned in triumph from battle, bringing booty and prisoners to present to Amen-Re. In this temple, there are six pylons or gate-ways and these impressive structures give access to the various areas of the building. Other pylons (seven to ten) form part of a processional avenue which leads to the nearby Temple of Mut, dedicated to Amun's consort. The ninth and tenth pylons were built by Horemheb, the last ruler of the Eighteenth dynasty; here infill blocks were incorporated from nearby demolished temples dedicated to the sun-disc, Aten, by Pharaoh Akhenaten, and we shall return to the significance of these blocks later.

In the Great Temple of Amun, there were various smaller sanctuaries built by different rulers. These included the temple of Ramesses III, an example of a classical Egyptian temple and the Great Hypostyle Hall, built mainly by Sethos I and his son Rames-ses II. This was one of the wonders of antiquity and today, with its soaring columns, it is an impressive and awe-inspiring sight. Here, on the walls, scenes depict the king's campaigns in Palestine and Syria. In the Central Court, where four obelisks were originally erected by Tuthmosis I and Tuthmosis III in the Eighteenth dyn-asty, only one – that of Tuthmosis I – still remains. In the Small Hall, there is a reminder of Hatshepsut, the formidable queen regnant of the Eighteenth dynasty who seized the throne from her young step-son, Tuthmosis III, claiming that she inherited her right to rule Egypt from her divine father Amen-Re. Here, she erected two pink granite obelisks to celebrate her jubilee festival. They were later enclosed to hide them from view by Tuthmosis III when he ousted his step-mother from power and became king. The right-hand obelisk has fallen but the other remains standing.

Other major areas include the Sanctuary of the Sacred Barques and the Great Festival Hall of Tuthmosis III; a small hall leads off this which is noteworthy for its unusual wall decoration – the reliefs show the variety of plants and animals which were collected on one of Tuthmosis III's campaigns in Syria and brought back to Egypt. The Temple of Amun has a feature which is common to all temples – its sacred lake is still in existence, and on the edge of this, there remains a large granite scarabeus mounted on a pedestal which Amenophis III dedicated to the form of the sun-god known as Atum-Khepri.

Between the ninth and tenth pylons, there is another court with a small temple of Amenophis II on the east side. Beyond the tenth pylon, to the south of Amenophis's temple, an avenue of ram-headed sphinxes leads to the Temple of Mut. Dedicated to the wife of Amun, this is the second largest temple of the complex, and, like several others, was originally a separate sanctuary which was later incorporated in Amun's vast complex. This temple is typical of the New Kingdom type, except for a horse-shoe shaped lake. The ruined temples of Amenophis III and Ramesses III are nearby.

Another avenue of sphinxes joins the Temple of Mut with the main processional way which linked the Karnak complex with the southern Temple of Luxor, which was known as the 'Southern Harim'. This temple was built by Amenophis III and dedicated to Amun, Mut and Khonsu; Tutankhamun completed the work, and Ramesses II made later additions. It was regarded as the sanctuary and home of Mut, Amun's wife and consort, and each year, he made a journey to Luxor from his own temple at Karnak. This was the occasion for a great festival, known as the 'Festival of Opet', which is depicted in scenes on the walls of the Colonnade in the Temple of Luxor. The procession would have taken the route from the south gate of the Temple of Karnak, along the great avenue, to the entrance on the northern side of the Temple of Luxor. It takes little imagination to conjure up from the Luxor scenes the excitement of this occasion, as the statue of the god was carried high in his golden barque by the white-robed priests. There would be clamour and shouting as the fervent worshippers pressed in on all sides and the procession would be accompanied by chanting and singing and dancing. The priests who preceded the barque would purify the god's way by wafting incense, and finally, the entourage would reach its destination. The god's statue would enter the temple where his divine wife awaited him, and outside the walls of the temple, the people would continue with their festivities for a period of twenty-four days, at the end of which time the god's statue would be brought back again to Karnak.

There were several other small but important temples in the Karnak complex. One was the temple dedicated to Khonsu which

Ramesses III initiated; this lies to the west of the Great Temple of Amun and it is a typical example of a New Kingdom temple. To the north of the great Amun temple, there were two temples dedicated to Ptah (built by Tuthmosis III) and Montu built by Amenophis III). Such subsidiary temples within the complex were dedicated either to members of Amun's own family, or to other gods whose former importance or close association with the area might have threatened Amen-Re's supremacy. Thus, the great creator-god Ptah and Montu, the deity who had originally been worshipped at Thebes, were both brought under Amen-Re's supervision.

The staffing of this great complex was an important feature of Egyptian society which had repercussions far beyond the confines of the temple and its estates. The priesthood here received a large proportion of the income from the god's estates as payment for their services, and they formed a wealthy and envied class. Such privileges attracted the most able and ambitious men in the country. The temple seems to have been administered as a department of the royal administration, nominally under the king, and the supervision and organization of the temple, its personnel and estates was apparently mostly entrusted to senior government officials. The vizier during the reign of Tuthmosis III, a man named Rekhmire, seems to have been held responsible for the organization and supervision of the whole economy of the Temple of Karnak. Scenes and inscriptions in his Theban tomb make this evident, and the duties and responsibilities listed there, for which he was nominally answerable (although many of them would undoubtedly have been delegated), are awesome in their diversity.

At the top of the temple hierarchy was the High Priest of Amun; men who held this post were usually high-ranking courtiers who attained this important position as the result of an outstanding political career at the royal Court rather than by progressing through the various levels of the temple priesthood. These men had great political power at their disposal and their support for a ruler could be essential to his holding on to the throne. Their influence was also reflected in their ownership of great estates and houses and a large staff of organizers and servants.

Under the High Priest, who was also known as the 'First Prophet' of the god, came the highest rank of clergy who were referred to as the 'fathers of the god'; these included the second, third and fourth prophets of Amun. The ordinary priests followed; they were called w'bw (wabau), a title which signified that they were ritually and bodily 'pure', having cleansed themselves in the Sacred Lake. Other priests were specialists in different branches of learning which were required in the temple – such as the liturgy, astronomy and astrology, and music. The rituals were probably accompanied in part by singing and dancing and women served in the temples in both capacities. Some of these women at least appear to have been ladies of rank, for the mummies and coffins and funerary equipment of some of the 'Chantresses of Amun' are very fine.

It seems that the members of the priesthood who held the top positions at Karnak were probably employed there on a full-time basis, but that, as elsewhere, the lower grades served in the temple on a regular but temporary basis, being divided into four groups, each of which served in the temple annually for three periods of one month.

Amen-Re was obviously a mighty and victorious deity whose claim to be Egypt's national god was unrivalled at this time. However, it is perhaps more intriguing to consider the other side of his nature as a helper of the poor, protector of the weak, loving father, and incorruptible judge who treated rich and poor equally. Although architecture, artefacts and literature underline the power of the state cult in Egypt, evidence of personal piety is harder to trace. People undoubtedly prayed to deities such as Bes and Tauert whose statuettes would have adorned many household shrines. Prayers would have been offered up to the deity for help or guidance in personal problems. The effect of the state-gods – remote in their great temples – upon the daily lives of the people was probably very limited, and it is therefore particularly surprising to discover that Amen-Re, the most powerful and universal of all the state-gods, also inspired worship on a much humbler level.

At Thebes, the god – in his earlier form of Amun – had been the local deity long before his rise to fame in the New Kingdom. This special relationship between Amun and the people of Thebes is well illustrated in the community which, during the New Kingdom, lived in the village known today as Deir el-Medina. This was built for the workmen (and their families) who were employed in the decoration of the royal tombs in the Valley of the Kings and The Valley of the Queens. The village lies on the west bank of the river, some distance from the royal burial places, in a desolate region. A thick wall – built with mudbricks which are stamped with the name of King Tuthmosis I – encloses about seventy dwelling houses; the village also possesses a temple and a nearby cemetery where the dead were placed in family tombs. Some of these tombs were very elegant and even incorporated miniature pyramids on top of the funerary chapels, at a time when the royal burials no longer used this device. These pyramids have no direct connection with the sun-cult being purely decorative in function, even if somewhat ostentatious for the tombs of workmen.

Deir el-Medina is one of only a small number of sites which have been excavated where people lived and worked. Other villages of this type which were occupied by workmen decorating and building a royal tomb or pyramid have been uncovered at Kahun (for the men who built the Middle Kingdom pyramid at Lahun in the Fayoum) and at Amarna (near to the city and necropolis built for the heretic Pharaoh Akhenaten at the end of the Eighteenth dynasty). Others almost certainly existed and perhaps await discovery. The Theban rulers used the Valley of the Kings for their burials for many generations, throughout the Eighteenth, Nineteenth and Twentieth dynasties, and Deir el-Medina was probably occupied throughout this time by the workmen involved not only in the decoration of the king's tomb, but also the repair and maintenance of older royal tombs.

The tombs were actually carved out of the cliffs or mountains by another workforce – the heavy labourers who were made up of convicted criminals, prisoners-of-war, and men conscripted by the government who were paid subsistence during the period of their employment.

These men were not to be confused with the highly skilled craftsmen of Deir el-Medina. Their task was to decorate the interior walls of the royal tombs with the brightly painted scenes which can be seen there today. When the royal tomb was completed, they commenced work on the tombs of favourite queens and princes and even of high-ranking courtiers. Nevertheless they were able to increase their standard of living by using some of their time and a great deal of their skill for private work, producing exquisite trinkets and toilet articles for their wealthy clients. Fathers passed the secrets of their trades on to their sons in this close-knit community, and the families were able to devote some of their additional wealth to the preparation of their own tombs.

The village, now much ruined, is of a substantial but un-imaginative design. Like other villages of the same type, it is organized in rows of terraced houses, and was probably devised and set out by the royal architect. The village rubbish-heaps have proved a rich source of information regarding the life and  workings of the village. Inscribed limestone and pottery sherds, thrown into the heaps, have been rescued and studied; the mass of material has brought to light facts about business transactions, inheritances, crimes and judgments, and the organization of the work-men and their payment.

The artisans followed a variety of trades; there were quarrymen, carpenters, sculptors and painters, and they came under the overall supervision of the Royal Scribe. They worked in a gang consisting of about sixty men, divided into two sections which were em-ployed simultaneously on the two sides of the tomb; each side was directed by a foreman and his deputy. A diary, kept by the scribe, recorded details of each day's work, including reasons given for absence, problems and complaints, and this was regularly submit-ted to the vizier. The men worked an eight-hour day and were accommodated in rest-shelters near the site of the tomb. The village was some distance from the necropolis and so they returned to the village only for the regular monthly rest days on the tenth, twentieth and thirtieth days and for the festivals. Their tools were provided and they received payment in kind – grain, barley and occasional extra luxuries such as wine, salt cakes, natron, meat and Asiatic beer.

The village community had an amazing degree of self-government; the workmen acted as priests in the village shrines and the local law-court was made up of villagers who settled all their own legal matters and disputes, only passing a case to the vizier if it involved capital punishment, when his ratification had to be obtained.

Some of the ostraca are decorated with sketches which give a fleeting glimpse of the wry sense of humour which these artisans possessed; this private 'art' is far removed from the traditional art in the tombs, although it was produced by the same artists. Carica-tures, quickly sketched by the artists on one of their rest days in the village and then tossed into the nearest rubbish heap, express an originality which is not found in the tomb and temple art. In some drawings, the characters are depicted in animal form, the nobility being shown as mice and the servants, ever attentive to the mice, as cats. That the residents of Deir el-Medina were well aware of the importance of their skills to their social superiors is very evident.

By the Twentieth dynasty, there was great social unrest in Egypt, and general poverty and discontent led to increased crime and tomb robbery. Lack of grain in the granaries meant that the workmen's rations became long overdue, and during the last years of Ramesses III (c. 1165 BC), the workmen, dissatisfied with the delay in payment, took industrial action – the first such protest which has come to light. It was essential that the men should complete the Royal Tomb before the king's death, and special action had to be taken to ensure that they returned to their task. The efforts of the vizier to obtain food supplies for the men and the delivery of the food finally persuaded them to resume work.

Deir el-Medina was an interesting community in both political and social terms, but it was also the place where Amen-Re was worshipped as a personal deity. The village was founded by Amenophis I, one of the earliest rulers of the Eighteenth dynasty and the first king to be buried in the Valley of the Kings. He was particularly revered by the people of Deir el-Medina and was even worshipped as a god although the deification of a king or of a man was extremely rare in Egypt; kings were usually only worshipped collectively as the ancestors of the living pharaoh because their support of the ruler and his right to reign was regarded as essential.

The mottoes found on scarabs worn by the ordinary people here explicitly praise Amen-Re and he was obviously the deity to whom their prayers and requests were addressed. He is hailed as the 'Lord of Life' by one petitioner, others claim 'My heart has no refuge than Amun', or 'Amen-Re is the strength of the lonely'.

Even in the official hymns to Amun we see his role as champion of the poor and insiginificant man. In the Great Hymn addressed to him, Amun is described as –

He who heareth the prayer of the prisoner; kindly of heart when one calleth to him. He who rescueth the fearful from the oppressor, who judgeth between the miserable and the strong.

Or in shorter hymns –

Amun, lend thine ear to one that standeth alone in the court, that is poor, and his (adversary) is rich.

. . . it is found that Amun changeth himself into the vizier, in order to cause the poor man to overcome. It is found that the poor man is justified and that the poor (passeth) by the rich.

Another hymn emphasizes the incorruptible nature of the god –

He taketh not unrighteous reward, and he speaketh not to him that bringeth testimony, and looketh not on him that maketh promises.

Amen-Re retained his appeal for the ordinary people even after the Thebans gave him supreme status as a national god with influence extending beyond Egypt to her empire in Nubia and Asia Minor. However, towards the end of the Eighteenth dynasty, the relationship between the god and the line of kings became increasingly strained. The kings felt their authority threatened in the same way as rulers towards the end of the Old Kingdom must have done when the cult of Re and its powerful priesthood came to rival the king. In the New Kingdom, the wealth of the king was greater than that of Amen-Re; in theory, the king alone could perform the rituals for the god and his priests were merely delegates appointed by the king. A strong ruler could keep the reins of power firmly in his own hands. However, in the Eighteenth dynasty, although many of the rulers were determined and even aggressive rulers, there was family conflict over the right of succession, and here the High Priest of Amun had great power. He could probably exert his influence over the selection of the next ruler when controversy arose, and express or withhold divine approval. He would almost certainly have taken the side of one rival against another when such situations came about.

It was during the long reign of Amenophis III, which spanned much of the later part of the Eighteenth dynasty, that the king began to take limited steps to contain the power of the priesthood of Amen-Re. Egypt's position of authority in Asia Minor was now assured and she could relax and enjoy the spoils of conquest. The real religious upheaval eventually occurred in the time of Amenophis IV, the son and successor of Amenophis III. He sought to destroy, once and for all, the might of Amen-Re and his priesthood and to replace it with a form of solar monotheism.

# 8    *The Disc of the Sun*

The young prince who was to become Egypt's most controversial ruler grew up at Thebes in surroundings which were luxurious even by Egyptian standards of elegance and beauty. His father, King Amenophis III, enjoyed a long reign over a land which had reached the height of its prosperity and which wielded considerable influence abroad. Although the seeds of destruction were already present in Egypt's relationships with other states in Asia Minor, outwardly at least the country flourished and was acknowledged the most powerful in the area. Foreign royalty sought to persuade the Egyptian king to take their princesses as wives and certainly some of these ladies with their retinues and presents for Pharaoh entered Egypt at this time. Indeed, the political and diplomatic links with bordering countries paved the way for an influx of foreign ideas and people which resulted in a decidedly cosmopolitan society.

Amenophis III seems to have delighted in his thriving country and to have enjoyed the pleasures of a rich and powerful ruler. He carried out an extensive building programme, and commenced work on a fine temple to Amun, Mut and Khonsu at Luxor, known today as the Temple of Luxor. He made additions to the Temple of Karnak and he built a vast mortuary temple on the wide plain on the west side of the river at Thebes. Regrettably only two enormous statues of the king survive from this temple, which was probably the largest such edifice ever erected. The temple was probably demolished during the Nineteenth dynasty, being a tempting source of building material. The statues, known as the 'Colossi of Memnon', mark the site of the original temple.

This king and his favourite wife, Tiye, probably inspired a

divine cult. At Soleb, he dedicated a temple to himself and to Amun, and in later texts, he is named with Ptah as a god of Memphis.

He built a vast palace complex on the west bank at Thebes, south of the place where the Temple of Medinet Habu now stands, at a site known today as Malkata. This covered over eighty acres of land which fringed the desert edges; the complex consisted of a series of one storey buildings which were built of mud-brick and then plastered and painted. To the east of these buildings there was a large T-shaped lake. The 'palace' in fact resembled a city and this was essentially its function – to provide the royal family with a place of residence and to accommodate all the administrative quarters necessary for administering the royal business. It was founded in or before Year eleven of the king's reign and was called 'House-of-Nebmaetre (is) the Splendour of Aten'. It included several separate royal dwellings – the King's Palace, the South Palace (which his favourite wife, Queen Tiye, perhaps used), the Middle Palace (Amenophis IV may have lived here with his family during his final years at Thebes), and the North Palace (which was probably built for another important member of his family – possibly his daughter, Sitamun, whom he also married).

Other areas were taken up with administrative quarters, the houses of senior palace officials, servants and minor attendants, as well as the harem or women's quarters where the many lesser royal wives and concubines were accommodated. Some of the chambers in the complex were decorated with delightful scenes depicting the flora and fauna of the countryside, painted on to the plastered walls. Here, unrestricted by religious traditions and conventions, the artists had a freer hand than in the tombs, and some of the motifs at Malkata appear to have an eastern Mediterranean origin which suggests that foreign workmen were employed to decorate parts of the complex.

Here, then, Prince Amenophis lived as a boy, the child of Amenophis III by his Great Royal Wife, Queen Tiye. He was one of several children born to this couple, although his father doubtless had many other children by his various wives. Amenophis was not, however, the heir to the throne, for his elder brother Thutmose was expected to succeed Amenophis III, but the old king was long-lived and Thutmose died before him. Of their other children, of whom there were at least five daughters, Prince Amenophis was chosen by his father to become his successor.

Amenophis III was himself the son of King Tuthmosis IV and his Great Royal Wife, Mutemweya. Previous kings of the Eighteenth dynasty had consolidated their claim to the throne by marrying the royal heiress, usually their own sister or half-sister, but by the time of Tuthmosis IV's accession, the dynastic conflicts within this family had largely ceased. It became more important perhaps to cement relationships with a foreign power by marrying a foreign princess, or, even at this early date, it is possible that the king was attempting to curb the influence of the priesthood of Amun. The priests had previously played a considerable role in determining the selection of Egypt's king and their patronage was very important to the contenders. They would have supported the traditional marriage between royal heir and heiress and the king's abandonment of such a tradition may have been an attempt to show the priests that he, the king, could establish any pattern of marriage that he chose and could also dictate that the children of such a marriage would be the legitimate heirs to the throne. Whatever the reason behind this change of policy, Tuthmosis IV married a Mitannian princess, Mutemweya, whom he made his principal queen and the mother of his heir.

The son of this union, Amenophis III took this one stage further by marrying not only a woman who was not related to him, but one who was not even royal. His choice was Tiye, whose father, Yuya, was a Prophet of Min and superintendent of the god's cattle at Akhmim, and whose mother was named Thuya. Yuya also became the king's 'Overseer of Horses', and he adopted the title of 'god's father' which may have had the significance of 'king's father-in-law'. Amenophis III issued a series of commemorative scarabs during his reign to mark important events and the first of these celebrated his marriage to Tiye; the inscription on these scarabs in fact underlines the non-royal origin of his bride's parents.

The marriage has obviously been of considerable interest to historians. One theory is that Yuya and Thuya were of foreign stock – possibly Nubian or Libyan, but it is now generally believed that they were Egyptians. Tiye was not their only child; her brother was named 'A-nen. He was the Second Prophet of the Four Chief Prophets of Amun and the Greatest of Seers in the Temple of Re-Atum during the reign of Amenophis III and he possessed a tomb-chapel in western Thebes. It has also been suggested that Tiye may have had another brother – Ay, who later

25 Cartonnage mummy mask

26 Pair-statue of man and wife from tomb

27 Wax painted portrait overlying face of mummy

28 Temple of Karnak –
avenue of ram-headed
sphinxes

29 Temple of Karnak –
seated statue of lion-headed
goddess, Sekhmet

30 Deir el-Medina – general view of workmen's village

31 Deir el-Medina – close-up of reconstructed miniature pyramid on one of workman's tombs

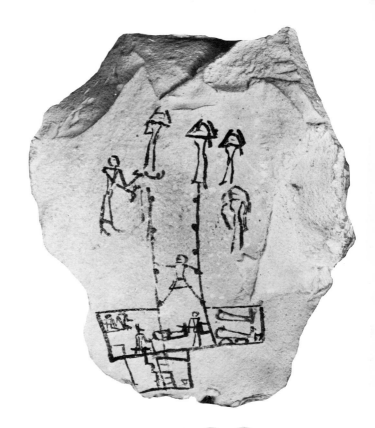

32 Limestone ostracon showing funeral. New Kingdom

33 Faience amulet of Bes, a popular household god

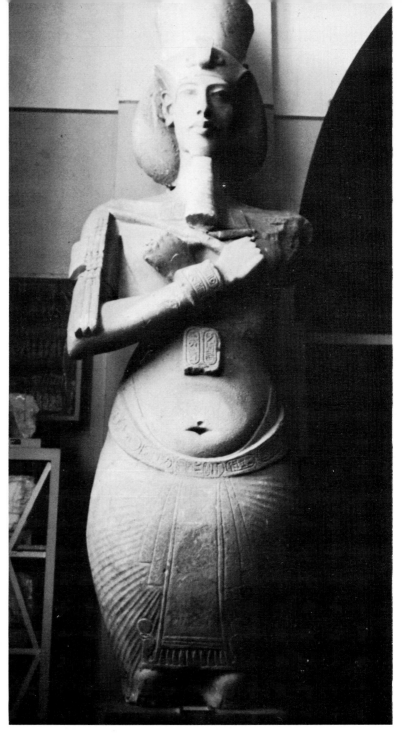

34 Large statue of Akhenaten from Aten Temple at Thebes, in Cairo Museum

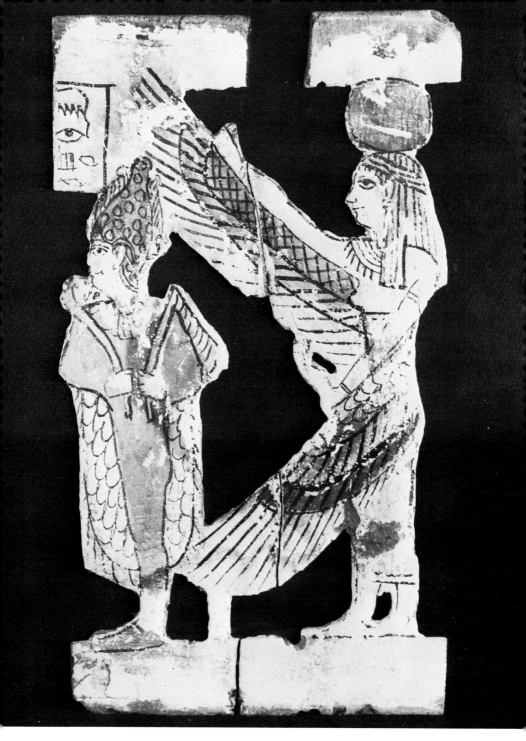

35 Wooden panel showing Osiris and Isis

36 Part of cartonnage head and chest cover. Graeco-Roman period

became the vizier of Tutankhamun and eventually, for a short time, king of Egypt. This idea is based on the similarity of the names of Yuya and Ay and of the titles and positions which both men are known to have held. Ay was 'Overseer of all the horses of his Majesty' in the reign of Amenophis IV, and, like Yuya, referred to himself as 'One trusted by the good god (the king) in the entire land', 'praised by the good god' and 'foremost of the companions of the king'. Ay also had close family connections with Akhmim, the town where he erected a shrine to the god Min and recorded a long inscription. Like Yuya, Ay held the title of 'god's father' and he was the only courtier to be thus addressed during the reign of his king, Amenophis IV. It has also been suggested that Nefertiti, the wife and principal queen of Amenophis IV, may have been the daughter of Ay. If this is a correct supposition, then Yuya and Ay, father and son, would have provided wives, Tiye and Nefertiti, for two successive rulers, Amenophis III and his son, Amenophis IV. Such a close relationship with these kings would explain the importance which Ay continued to wield at Court over a period of many years.

Despite her non-royal origin, or perhaps because of it, Tiye attained the highest position amongst the king's wives. Amenophis III soon associated her name with his in royal inscriptions and made her his Great Royal Wife. Her parents were also granted an unprecedented privilege: although commoners, they were provided with a small but richly endowed tomb in the otherwise exclusively royal Valley of the Kings, which Theodore M. Davis, the American archaeologist, discovered in 1905. It had been robbed in antiquity, but still contained tomb goods and the mummies of Yuya and Thuya. Tiye retained her powerful position at Court and Amenophis III ensured that her son became his heir. The extent of her influence on her son has been much discussed but a woman of her obvious strength and purpose was undoubtedly a force in palace circles and in steering the ambitions of her own children.

Tiye was however not the only wife of Amenophis III. Indeed, in addition to the many women of Egyptian origin who lived in his harem, the king followed his father's custom of cementing foreign alliances by marriage. In Year ten of his reign, he married Gilukhepa, the daughter of Shuttarna the king of Mitanni, a state in Asia Minor which was of considerable political importance at this time. Shuttarna's daughter arrived in Egypt accompanied by

317 female attendants, and the event was recorded on a set of commemorative scarabs; even on these, the names of Tiye and her parents are honoured by being placed immediately after that of the king. When Tushratta succeeded his father as king of Mitanni, negotiations were once again started between him and Amenophis III who wished to marry another princess of the family – this time, Tadukhipa, Tushratta's daughter. She was eventually sent to Egypt with many fine gifts, to become the new queen of Amenophis III, although he was by now an aging and sickly man. The families continued to treat each other with respect and friendship even after the old king's death, for Tushratta wrote to the widowed Tiye, expressing the hope that the good relations which had existed in the past would continue in the reign of her son. Tiye was quite obviously a great authority at the Egyptian Court and was treated as such by foreign royalty. The royal harem of Amenophis III also included at least one sister of the king of Babylonia, and the king married Sitamun, his own daughter by his favourite wife Tiye, before the thirty-first year of his reign, and gave her the additional title of 'King's Chief Wife'. This again broke with the tradition of brother-sister marriages in the royal family, for Sitamun might have been regarded as the most suitable wife for her own brother and the successor to the throne, Amenophis IV. The possible role of Sitamun as the mother of two other sons of Amenophis III – Tutankhamun and Smenkhkare – may have been behind this move.

Amenophis IV married Nefertiti, the queen whose very name has become associated with great beauty through her portrayals in the art of the period. Her origins are completely obscure. At one time, scholars suggested that she could be identified with the Mitannian princess Tadukhipa who had entered the harem of Amenophis III in his declining years. It was thought possible that the princess was then given to his son in marriage. Since she never asserts herself as 'King's Daughter' or 'King's Sister' in any existing inscriptional evidence, it would appear that she was not the daughter of Amenophis III or the sister of Amenophis IV. Apart from her title of queen, she claims only to be 'heiress', which was a title also used by her mother-in-law Queen Tiye. It has been suggested that she too was of non-royal parents but that her father was perhaps a prominent courtier. Ay, the 'god's father', who was a man of great importance in the reign of Amenophis IV (and was possibly the brother of Tiye), is the most likely candidate. Ay's

wife was named Tey, and again, the similarity between the names
of Thuya, Tiye and Tey is a possible indication that the women
were closely related. Tey, however, was apparently not the
mother of Nefertiti, for her titles indicate only that she was Nefertiti's nurse or tutor. In his eventual tomb, Ay is shown only with
one wife, Tey, but it is feasible that he was previously married to
the mother of Nefertiti and that she may have died, perhaps in
childbirth, but such theories are speculative. We do know, however, that Nefertiti had a sister. She appears as lady-in-waiting to
the queen in the royal retinue depicted in tomb scenes at the new
site of El-Amarna, the city and burial area constructed by Nefertiti's husband. Here she is described as 'queen's sister', and she is
also prominent in the wall-scenes in Ay's tomb. Her name was
Mutnodjme. The last king of the Eighteenth dynasty, Horemheb,
who had no royal blood, also had a wife of this name. Some
scholars maintain that this is the same woman whom he married
to support his claim to the throne.

One aspect of this period which has been much disputed centres
around a possible co-regency between Amenophis III and his son,
Amenophis IV. Some believe that Amenophis III shared his
throne with the younger king for as long as twelve years; others
consider it to have lasted for only a few months, and others argue
that it should be discounted altogether and that Amenophis IV
succeeded to the throne only upon his father's death. The system
of co-regency was not new at this time; the kings of the Middle
Kingdom had used it extensively when, in a period of political
instability and uncertainty, they wished to ensure the smooth
passage of the succession by taking as co-rulers their chosen heirs.
If the co-regency did exist between Amenophis III and his son, it
would have been understandable, for the senior king may well
have wished to establish the claim of his heir so that the priesthood
of Amen-Re would have less opportunity to support any rival
claimant put forward against the son of the non-royal Queen Tiye.

The debate as to whether or not there was such a co-regency
will doubtless continue, but the latest year date we have for
Amenophis III, based on the evidence of dockets from his palace at
Malkata, is his thirty-eighth regnal year and Amenophis IV ruled
Egypt for some seventeen years, these may have been years of
his sole or shared rule. It is also possible that Queen Tiye herself
may have exerted considerable power for at least a few months
between the reigns of father and son.

If the co-regency did exist, it would almost certainly have been spent at Thebes, where perhaps both kings occupied palaces at Malkata simultaneously. During this period, the final years at Thebes, we can see the beginnings of the religious revolution which was soon to engulf Egypt. The cult at the centre of this upheaval was that of the Aten, or sun's disc, and at one time, scholars regarded Amenophis IV as the originator of this deity believing that he was solely responsible for the religious reforms and new art forms, as well as the loss of most of Egypt's empire in Asia Minor. This viewpoint has since been modified as it is clear that many of the elements were already present in Egypt at least during the reign of his father and possibly at an even earlier period.

The cult which Amenophis IV raised to a position of unprecedented power was based on the worship of the life-force present in the sun. The solar cult had of course dominated Egyptian religious beliefs from at least the Old Kingdom, but the Egyptians had always worshipped the sun itself – the material body – which gave life and bounty to Egypt, and this had never been in any sense an exclusive cult for they had given homage to a multitude of deities. Amenophis IV, however, attempted to impose a religious faith which has loosely been described as a form of solar monotheism.

It is difficult to determine when the Aten (*itn*) – the disc of the sun – came to be revered as a separate entity. Mention of the Aten occurs as early as the Middle Kingdom, when in a passage from the text known as the 'Story of Sinuhe' it states – 'As for the king, he went up to heaven, being joined with Aten, the body of the god being united with him who made him.'

During the Eighteenth dynasty, when Egypt first came into contact with other countries and peoples, they naturally wished to give their own gods extended and 'international' powers, to see them as deities who could influence the lives of people in countries which Egypt wished to subdue. We have already seen that Amen-Re acquired such attributes and was regarded by the Egyptians as a universal god with responsibilities and creative powers beyond Egypt's own boundaries. Any god wishing to displace Amen-Re would have had to accentuate this aspect of his own cult.

The Aten certainly gained in stature during the early part of the Eighteenth dynasty, but it is not until the reign of Tuthmosis IV that the Aten was identified as a solar deity in its own right rather than as yet another form of the sun-god. This distinct form first occurs in the inscription on a scarab dated to this reign.

During Amenophis III's reign, however, references to the Aten increase and other evidence suggests that a cult was now established. The role of Amenophis III in promoting this cult and his reasons for so doing have been the subject of much scholarly discussion. Some Egyptologists believe that he provided the impetus for the new cult and was probably the instigator of the plan to promote the deity as a rival to Amen-Re and his priesthood. The name of the Aten certainly occurs more frequently – the royal barge was called the 'Splendour of the Aten', as was one of the king's regiments, and his palace was given the name of 'The House-of-Nebmaetre (is) the splendour of the Aten'. The prominence of the word 'Aten' in Beketaten – the name of Tiye's youngest daughter – may have been public affirmation that Amenophis III supported the cult which his son was apparently promoting.

Nevertheless Amenophis III did not neglect the cults of other gods; he honoured them with buildings as magnificent as any that his predecessors had endowed, and there is certainly no suggestion that he regarded Aten as a special deity to be singled out from the Egyptian pantheon.

During the early years of his adulthood at Thebes, Amenophis IV began to take practical steps in support of the Aten cult. He still retained his traditional royal name Amenophis (which meant 'Amun is satisfied') and at least outwardly respected the great god of Thebes, Amen-Re. However, he had also erected at Thebes a number of buildings, including temples, in honour of the Aten, and for this, he must have used some of the revenue in his father's treasury.

A recent study of these buildings has brought a new dimension to the scholars' view of this period. The buildings were dismantled by later rulers, and the blocks used to fill in later constructions at Thebes, notably the Temples of Karnak and Luxor. In AD 1893 a scholar noted the existence of such blocks but it was not until many years afterwards, when the later constructions were themselves being dismantled, that some thirty-six thousand decorated blocks from the Aten temples at Thebes were revealed.

The study of this vast number of blocks has been undertaken since 1966 by the Akhenaten Temple Project of the University Museum, University of Pennsylvania, and has involved photographing, studying and piecing together into relief scenes the thousands of sandstone blocks. This giant jig-saw puzzle has obviously posed considerable problems, and the team of experts were faced with a variety of difficulties. Most of this masonry had been removed from the later buildings with no record of the original location of each block. Subsequently, in their temporary storehouse, the blocks had been moved around at random, creating further confusion. In addition a number of the *talatat* (the small sandstone blocks with standard dimensions of $52 \times 22 \times 26$ cms) had been stolen and exported from Egypt and had ended up in private collections and museums in the U.S.A. and in western Europe.

To assist them in their mammoth task, the project made novel use of the computer, without which the volume of work would have been impossible to contemplate. Aided by the computer, it has been possible to match up to thirty-five thousand elements of this great puzzle, and store the relevant data permanently at the computer centre where it can be recalled at any time.

First the *talatat* in the storehouse situated at the modern town of Luxor, on the site of ancient Thebes, and additional blocks in collections outside Egypt were photographed to scale. Then the basic characteristics of the texture of the blocks and their decoration were noted on to computer cards. This was followed by computerization, and the classification and matching of some thirty-five thousand *talatat*. These represent only a fraction of the total number of blocks used to build the sun-temples at Thebes.

A book recently published gives an interim report on the research of the team: decorated blocks have provided new ideas and information on the royal family, priestly functionaries, secular officials, the jubilee festival and the royal palace as represented in the reliefs, but the future study of the blocks promises further insight.

It is still uncertain how many buildings were originally constructed from the *talatat*, but the evidence indicates that there were at least two temples – one at Karnak and the other at Luxor – and also possibly a ceremonial palace. Indeed, Akhenaten and Nefertiti may both have had separate temples built at Karnak. One of the most fascinating conclusions to emerge is that the queen had unprecedented importance in this cult and that great emphasis was placed on femininity in the reliefs. Indeed, the queen may have equalled her husband in the importance of her cult role, which would have been a considerable break with tradition. The blocks which depict this unique occurrence were apparently later defaced and placed upside down in the later buildings, probably at the wish of those instigating the religious counter-revolution of the succeeding reigns.

The research has also shown the importance and significance of the young king's early years at Thebes and the extent of his building activities. These facts were not previously fully appreciated, and indeed the strength of the Aten's presence at Thebes before the move to the new city of Akhetaten has never been so clearly indicated before. One aspect of future research is the proposed clearing of the area where these buildings were probably located with the aim of establishing their extent, nature and purpose.

However, despite the considerable advances made even at Thebes to promote the cult of the Aten, Amenophis IV seems to have considered that more drastic measures were necessary, perhaps because his relationship with the priests of Amen-Re at Thebes became increasingly difficult. They can hardly have welcomed the diversion of funds to the cult of the Aten or the proliferation of Aten buildings which now appeared in the very heart of their own deity's great cult centre. We do not know the steps which led to Akhenaten's dramatic solution, but in the fifth year of his reign, he undertook to establish an exclusive solar monotheistic cult in Egypt. To curtail the influence of the priests, he obliterated from the monuments the names of the many other deities, he removed the income from their temples and diverted it to the Aten, and he disbanded their priesthoods. He changed his name to Akhenaten (probably 'Servant of the Aten') and his queen, Nefertiti, added another name of Neferneferuaten (meaning 'Fair is the goddess of the Aten'). Thus, they publicly denounced any further association with Amen-Re. The king later added another title – 'Living in Truth' – which stressed his role as the upholder of the cosmic order.

An even greater break with tradition was achieved by moving his capital and religious centre away from Thebes and its old associations to a completely new city which he built mid-way between Thebes and the old northern centres in Lower Egypt. Fourteen large boundary stelae delineated the city and its environs and they are inscribed with an account of the founding and setting up of the city. The site was selected by the king, at the behest of the god, and the king promised that he would never extend the limits of the original area. He also asked that his body should be brought back to the site for burial if he should die elsewhere in Egypt, and that the same should be done for immediate members of his family.

The city was called 'Akhetaten' (meaning 'Horizon of the Aten') and it occupied a position between the river and the encircling sweep of the eastern mountains, following the course of the Nile for almost eight miles. Today, there is little to see of this once magnificent city which was as much the result of the religious zeal of its royal builder as the more famous pyramids at Gizeh built by the Fourth dynasty pharaohs. However, looking down on this wide plain from the rocky slopes where the nobles' tombs were built, it is still possible to imagine the palaces, villas, gardens, administrative headquarters, military barracks, records offices, and large roofless sun-temples, and to marvel that the city was put up and inhabited during the comparatively short reign of one king. Mostly constructed of plastered mud-brick, the walls of the royal palaces and private villas were covered with scenes of plants, flowers and animals reminiscent of the older, distant palace at Malkata where Akhenaten had lived previously. The pavements were also finely decorated with paintings of plants found in the lush cultivation area, and these were executed in delicate, muted shades. Further embellishments made use of tiles and polychrome faience inlays. However, despite its immediate beauty and elegance, the archaeologists discovered that the buildings were often hastily and poorly constructed.

In the cliffs to the east of the city there were rock-cut tombs, built and decorated for the eventual burial of the king and his entourage although in fact few were ever laid to rest here. Nevertheless the scenes carved on the walls of these tombs provide us with much of our information relating to this period. A village was also put up, to accommodate the work-force who constructed the city and the tombs.

Akhetaten was built on one bank of the river, but land was also reserved on the other side to grow the food supplies which a large community would require. The site was excavated by a number of expeditions, starting with that of Sir W. Flinders Petrie in 1891, and continuing under other British and German archaeologists until 1937, with a break during the period of the First World War. It was never completely excavated, and new work will shortly commence there. The site is often referred to as 'Tell el-Amarna' and indeed 'Amarna' has come to be a term applied not only to the site but more generally to the religion and art forms associated with this period of experimentation. However, Tell el-Amarna is a modern name which wrongly combines the name of the local village of El-Till with that of a nearby tribe, the Beni Amran, and 'El-Amarna' is now the preferred term.

At one time, it was believed that Akhenaten limited his activities to this site, but the name of Gem-Aten is known to have been given to an important place in Nubia, and the Aten buildings at Karnak and Luxor indicate that cult centres were in existence elsewhere. However, Akhetaten was definitely the main centre and the most important temples were built here. From the excavations at the site and from the representations of the temples found in some of the noble tombs at El-Amarna, it is apparent that there were several temples here, all built as sun-temples for the worship of the Aten. Like the Aten temples at Karnak, they appear to have constituted a break with tradition and to have had more in common with the solar temples of the Old Kingdom than with the cultus temples of the New Kingdom. Although further study of the layout of these temples and close examination of the scenes with which the temples at Karnak were decorated may eventually throw light on the exact nature of the rituals performed here, it is already apparent that the architecture of these sun-temples differed in several basic respects from the traditional structures. These temples had pylons and areas which led the worshipper through a series of enclosures towards the sanctuary where presumably the culmination of the rites took place. Unlike the other temples, these were unroofed, open to the sunlight, and enabled the god to be present to receive his offerings. Whereas the other temples gave protection to the god who resided in a cult statue, the Aten had no statue but his disc was visible in the heavens.

The ritual doubtless involved the presentation of food, flowers, and other offerings to the god by the person of the king, and possibly by other members of his family. These would have been placed on the many small altars set out in rows inside an area of the temple. The king's unique relationship with the god would have been exemplified and guaranteed by such rituals, and one of the first buildings which Akhenaten erected at his new site was the Great Temple to the Aten.

At Akhetaten, the king gathered around him courtiers who paid lip service to the new cult although the depth of their committal to

Aten's worship was probably superficial and motivated by desire for self-advancement. They were for the most part new men whom the king raised to positions of authority in return for their support. Only one is known to have accompanied him from Thebes – this was his butler, Parennufe, who built a tomb at Akhetaten – and there was of course his loyal courtier Ay, who became superintendent of the king's horses. Otherwise, support for the new faith was probably limited to members of the royal family.

Akhenaten's move to the new city need not be interpreted as a break between himself and his parents, Amenophis III and Tiye. Indeed, the couple may well have visited Akhetaten. Scenes in an Amarna tomb, belonging to a courtier, strongly suggest that the widowed Tiye, with Princess Baketaten, visited Akhenaten and Nefertiti in the new city, although it is uncertain whether the old queen actually took up residence there at the end of her life.

There were six daughters born to Akhenaten and Nefertiti, but there is no mention of a son. Of these, only two girls play a significant role in the history of the period – the eldest daughter, Meritaten, and the third one, Ankhesenpaaten. The second child, Maketaten, died shortly after her father's twelfth year of reign, and she was buried in a set of chambers leading off the main corridor of the royal tomb at Amarna. She was probably the only member of the royal family to occupy this tomb, although the bodies of her parents and sisters have in fact never been discovered. Scenes on the walls of the tomb show her family stricken with grief at the loss of their young princess. In one scene, a nurse is shown holding a baby, and various explanations of this have been suggested – perhaps Maketaten died in childbirth, or the baby belongs to either Nefertiti or Meritaten.

Amenophis III had married his own daughter Sitamun, and Akhenaten followed his example by taking not one but two of his own daughters as wives. Akhenaten first married his eldest daughter, Meritaten, and between the thirteenth and fifteenth years of his reign, Meritaten appears to replace her mother as his consort. The disappearance of Nefertiti from the foreground of royal life has been explained in various ways. Some scholars believe that she died soon after Maketaten's death and was perhaps originally buried in the Royal Tomb at El-Amarna; others consider that there was a rift between the king and his wife, perhaps over the religious revolution itself and the course it was taking, and that she

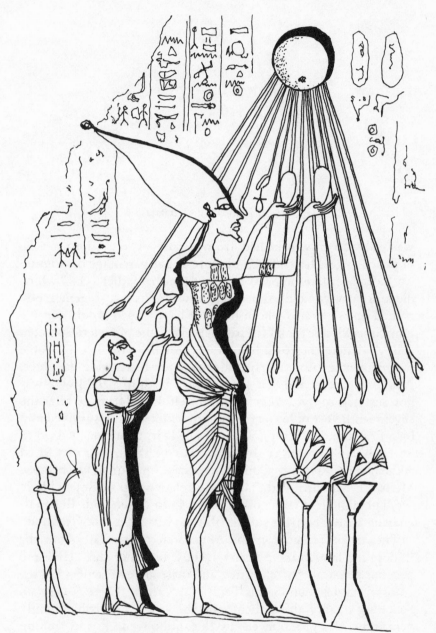

Figure 29 The ceremony of making offerings to the Aten

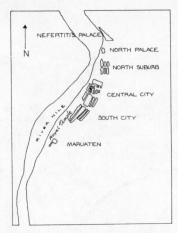

Figure 30 Plan of El-Amarna

was subsequently banished from Court or went into a self-imposed exile. Her end is as obscure as her parentage or origin.

Queen Meritaten appears to have borne her father a child which did not survive, and Akhenaten now took as co-regent a boy named Smenkhkare, whom he must have hoped would survive him. Smenkhkare took Nefertiti's special name of Neferneferuaten and Meritaten, the royal heiress, became his wife. It is probable that Akhenaten now married his next eldest surviving daughter, Ankhesenpaaten, and that she too gave birth to a child who was not destined to live. Akhenaten himself died during or after the seventeenth year of his reign, and Smenkhkare only survived him by a few months. With no direct male heir, the throne passed to Smenkhkare's younger brother, Tutankhaten, who married Akhenaten's widow, Ankhesenpaaten, presumably because Meritaten had also died. The exact relationship of Smenkhkare and Tutankhaten to each other, and also to Amenophis III and to Akhenaten, has been the subject of some very interesting research.

The art representations of Akhenaten which date from the middle and later years of his reign show him with distinctive and peculiar physical characteristics, and these are even evident in the colossal statues found in his Temple at Karnak. There is a certain brooding quality about them, and the king's face is hauntingly depicted with a pronounced jaw-line, hollow cheeks and slanting eyes, while his malformed body, with an excessively thin neck, broad hips and thighs and pronounced breasts, suggests that these features have been exaggerated almost to the point of caricature.

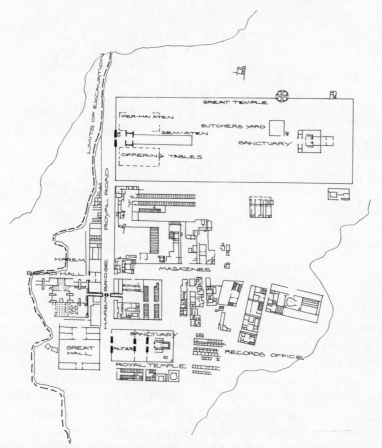

Figure 31 Plan of the Central City of El-Amarna

One statue shows the king with no genitalia; theological explanations of this have attempted to prove that the king is expressing the male and female qualities of the creator-god he represents on earth, but the interpretation is not totally convincing. The physical abnormalities also apply to portrayals of his family, and even on members of the king's entourage who had no familial connection and would not have inherited his characteristics. Akhenaten is always depicted wearing a crown, but his daughters are often shown with another peculiarity – distended skulls which may have also been passed on to them by their father.

Although the abnormalities were quickly transformed by Akhenaten's artists into an art form in their own right, with which loyal courtiers are also associated, the ailment from which the king probably suffered has been considered by various specialists. The

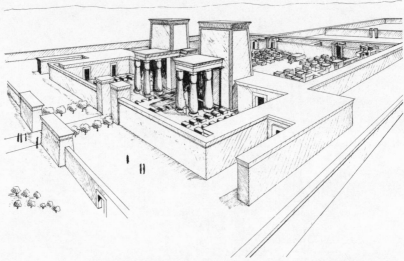

Figure 32 The Sanctuary of the Great Temple of the Aten at El-Amarna

body of the king, and those of his children, have never been found, so the theories have to be based on the evidence of the statuary and reliefs. An acceptable suggestion is that he suffered from a disorder of the endocrine gland, and perhaps specifically of the pituitary gland, a tumour of which can bring about a disorder known as Fröhlich's Syndrome. Features such as the distribution of fat in certain areas of the body and the retarded development of the genitalia can result from this Syndrome, which can also produce a form of hydrocephalus. One complication to this theory is that Fröhlich's Syndrome would probably have made him incapable of begetting children, and although one possibility is that Amenophis III could have fathered Akhenaten's 'daughters', it seems strange that a 'son' would not then have been produced for him to ensure succession. Without the body of Akhenaten, all discussion of this remains speculative.

The king's physical abnormality is particularly important in relation to the identification of a body found many years ago in the so-called 'Tomb of Tiye' which Theodore M. Davis located in the Valley of the Kings, and which is more commonly referred to as 'Tomb 55'. It had never been finished and the burial inside had been hastily performed; there was only one coffin instead of the customary nest of coffins inside the great sarcophagus, and some of the objects were found to be inscribed with Queen Tiye's name, sometimes accompanied by that of her husband, Amenophis III.

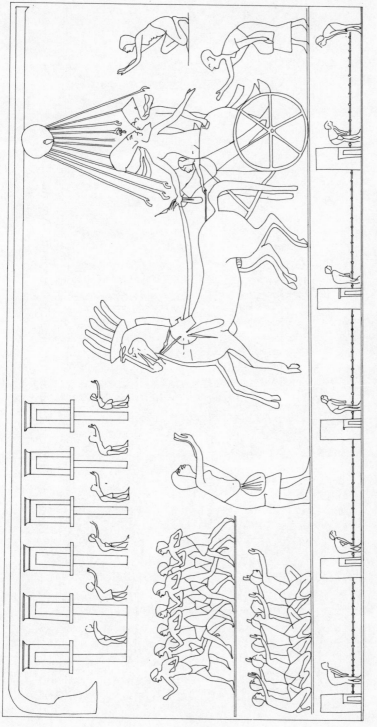

Figure 33 The Royal chariot passing the sentries, El-Amarna

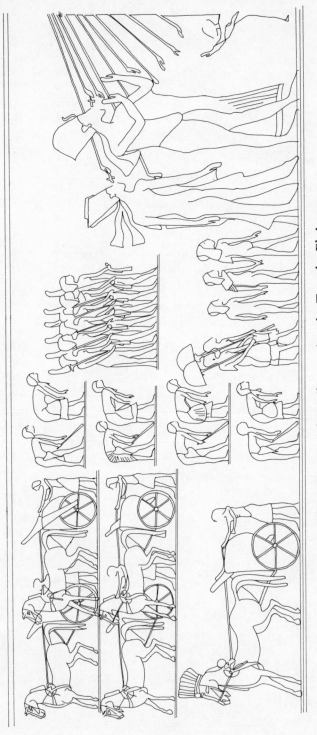

Figure 34 The Royal Family entering the Temple, El-Amarna

Particularly interesting was a shrine which had been reduced to its component parts, and which bore reliefs showing the queen and inscriptions recording that it had been made for her by Akhenaten; his actual name was defaced, but the context indicates that his name should be restored.

The identity of this body has since proved to be one of the most interesting controversies of the period. Because of its context, the body was first said to be that of Tiye herself, but a later opinion claimed that it was that of King Akhenaten and that it had been removed from El-Amarna to Thebes when Akhetaten was abandoned following the king's death.

Elliot Smith examined the body and claimed that it belonged to a young man of between twenty-three and twenty-five years of age, basing this on the fact that certain epiphyses had not yet united with their bones at the time of his death. Other scholars denied that all the events of Akhenaten's reign could have taken place in such a short lifetime. Elliot Smith then suggested that if Akhenaten had suffered from Fröhlich's Syndrome, he would be physically immature and that this body could in fact have belonged to a man aged about thirty-six years at the time of death.

Professor D. E. Derry later examined the body and he disagreed with Elliot Smith's conclusions, declaring that he could find no evidence of hydrocephalus, although the skull was of an unusual shape. He was convinced that this was the body of a young man of no more than twenty-three years, and he suggested that it belonged to Akhenaten's co-regent, Smenkhkare.

A later article by Sir Alan Gardiner proposed that the body belonged to neither man, but that the persons who had buried the body in Tomb 55 believed it to be that of King Akhenaten. As loyal followers of the king they had rescued the body from the ravaged royal tomb at El-Amarna where they had also found Akhenaten's coffin and the shrine he had dedicated to his mother. Having repaired the coffin and placed the body inside, they had re-buried it with an assortment of funerary goods in Tomb 55.

Professor H. W. Fairman believed the body to be that of Smenkhkare while C. Aldred favoured Akhenaten, although he too later identified it with the co-regent. However, the most recent examination of the body from Tomb 55 by Professor R. G. Harrison and Dr A. B. Abdalla and the subsequent examination of Tutankhamun's mummy produced fresh evidence. Not only did the bodies of the two young men show a marked anatomical similarity, but the body from Tomb 55 did not appear to resemble the statues of Akhenaten.

A reconstruction drawing, based on the skeletal evidence and other scientific data, of the head and face of the body in Tomb 55 showed a young man who closely resembled Tutankhamun but who barely resembled the gaunt appearance of Akhenaten's statues. A marked conformity was also found between the skulls and bones of the two young men, and the presence of holes in the humeri in both bodies indicated some degree of affinity. Finally, the tissues from both bodies were analysed, using a special serological micromethod devised by Connolly in 1969, to determine the blood groups of the mummies which were both found to be of the groups $A_2$ and MN. Each piece of evidence was perhaps not independently conclusive, but considered as a whole the known facts indicated that the bodies of Tutankhamun and of the person buried in Tomb 55 were those of close relatives. It is now generally accepted that these young men were probably full brothers and that the body in Tomb 55 belonged to Smenkhkare. The examination also concluded that Smenkhkare had probably died aged twenty, while his brother had been about nineteen at death. The highest regnal year which is known for Tutankhamun is year Ten, and for Smenkhkare, we have year Three, most of which time was probably spent in co-regency.

The parentage of these boys is as uncertain and as keenly disputed as most other aspects of the period. It is known that Tutankhaten (who later changed his name to Tutankhamun) was the son of a king, for an inscription on the Prudhoe lion in the British Museum collection claims that he '. . . renewed the monument of his father, King of Upper and Lower Egypt, Lord of the Two Lands, Nebmaetre, Image of Re, Son of Re, Amenophis, Ruler of Thebes'. Such a statement might mean that his father was Amenophis III, but some scholars have suggested that, since the word for 'father' can have a wider interpretation as 'ancestor' or more specifically as 'grandfather', the conclusion is not so simple, and that Tutankhaten could have been the son of Akhenaten. There is, however, much evidence against this, for, while Akhenaten is shown on many occasions in the company of his daughters, he is never credited with a son. It is most likely that both Smenkhkare and Tutankhaten were sons of Amenophis III.

The identity of their mother is again uncertain. Queen Tiye was by now well advanced in years and although she could have borne

Smenkhkare, it is unlikely that she could have been the mother of Tutankhaten. However, Sitamun, daughter of Amenophis III and Tiye, who married Amenophis III and became an important queen in her own right could have produced Amenophis III these sons. If this were the case, it is perhaps surprising that Tutankhamun was buried with objects which bore the name of Amenophis III and of Tiye, including a plait of her hair enclosed in its own small coffin, but with nothing belonging to Sitamun. It is of course feasible that the two boys were not born to a royal queen, and that they came from one of the many subsidiary branches of Amenophis III's family, their mother being a minor although perhaps favourite wife of the old king. The lack of direct and legitimate heirs from Akhenaten would have forced the royal family to draw his successors from the lower ranks of princes.

Smenkhkare is thought to have survived Akhenaten by perhaps a few months, and his premature death and apparent lack of an heir brought Tutankhaten to the throne. He was aged about nine years at the date of his accession and the influence of his royal advisers must have been considerable. Never had Egypt so desperately needed a strong ruler as at this period, and a succession of minor kings who died early and left no heir must have caused great misgivings at Court and elsewhere. The only stable factor was apparent in the person of Ay, the courtier of long-standing loyalty to the king, who now acted as chief adviser to the young ruler. Continuity was also provided by the marriage of Tutankhaten to Akhenaten's eldest surviving daughter and wife, Ankhesenpaaten, and this consolidated the young boy's claim to the throne. Unfortunately, this union also failed to produce healthy, male heirs, for the only evidence of their offspring is in the form of two mummified foetuses which were buried in his tomb.

Tutankhamun has become justifiably famous in modern times because in 1922, his tomb and its contents were discovered virtually intact, but in historical terms, his short reign is of interest mainly because it brought about the reversal of Akhenaten's religious upheaval and witnessed the re-instatement of the traditional deities. Before examining why a counter-revolution occurred so soon after Akhenaten's death and why it was apparently so easy to reverse the profound changes wrought in the brief time-span of his reign, we should first consider Akhenaten's motives and the effects which his actions had on Egypt in general.

Once Akhetaten had been discovered and evidence started to

come to light from a site which had been destroyed and hidden for thousands of years, the subject of the heretic king and his religious revolution became a favourite topic for historians, Biblical scholars, and popular writers. It has often been difficult to divorce this period of history from these writers' own Western, Christian background, and to consider it instead as part of the development of religion in Egypt, which is where it belongs. Such an attitude is most apparent in the works of older historians who regarded Akhenaten as an idealist, a 'failed Messiah', as the first reformer who tried, albeit unsuccessfully, to impose a form of monotheism on his people. They saw him as a philosopher who neglected his empire in Asia Minor while he pondered the concept of the Aten as a universal deity of love; a pacifist lord, in the isolation of his city at El-Amarna, supported by a beautiful queen who (evidence to the contrary not being available) appeared to be his only wife. The key factor which inspired such writers to eulogize Akhenaten as a great and far-sighted ruler sadly destined to failure was of course his so-called monotheism. This was seen not so much as the fanaticism of one ruler, or even as a development of existing trends in Egyptian religion, but rather as a truth revealed to one man whose brave efforts to communicate this to his subjects were cruelly curtailed by his own death and by the hostility of his one-time supporters.

The origin of his solar monotheism was disputed; it was thought possible that his mother Tiye was of foreign origin and that she had brought the cult of the Aten into Egypt and had encouraged her son in this worship; it was also suggested that the queen restrained him in the early years of his reign but was eventually unable to prevent him from making the Aten the Sole God and expunging the names of other deities. Others thought it likely that Mutemweya, queen of Tuthmosis IV, herself the daughter of a Mitannian king, could have brought new ideas with her which eventually flourished in the time of her grandson. A more direct influence on Prince Akhenaten would have been the royal court in which he grew to manhood, where princesses and their attendants came from lands far beyond Egyptian boundaries and doubtless brought a variety of faiths with them.

This view of a mystic and visionary king has been largely replaced in more recent years by the idea that Akhenaten was to some extent a political opportunist who introduced a new supreme deity in order to break the power of the priesthood of

Amen-Re and to return the king to his former position of unrivalled importance. Amun's priests certainly exploited their power and probably had considerable influence over most aspects of life in Egypt. Tuthmosis IV may have begun the attempt to curtail the priests' role long before. In his titles, Re and Atum are given prominence instead of Amun, and he was the first to break the tradition of marrying the royal heiress. However, there is no evidence to suggest any major break with Amun, and the same holds good for the reign of his son, Amenophis III, who, although he married a commoner and made her his Great Royal Wife and also gave increased prominence to the Aten, was nevertheless an orthodox ruler who paid due respect to Amen-Re.

Older historians credited Akhenaten with the introduction of monotheism and also with the creation of a cult dedicated to a hitherto unknown deity. This is now known to be inaccurate, for the Aten was mentioned as a god in at least the previous two reigns and it may well have been worshipped before that time. To Akhenaten, however, we can still apply the distinction that he alone of the Egyptian rulers can be shown to have made exclusive the cult of one god.

It was only during the New Kingdom that the priesthoods had achieved such political power and had become a truly professional body. The kings must have realised that they were gradually becoming bound by the wishes of the priesthoods. It was indeed a far cry from the early days of the Old Kingdom when the king had ruled his people on earth as the last of the gods and the first of men. The absolute authority which he held over his subjects is nowhere better expressed than in the pyramids which the rulers of the Fourth dynasty built on the plateau at Gizeh. By the New Kingdom, these royal tombs were already ancient monuments – a testimony to the early kings' supreme power achieved under the patronage of the old sun-god, Re when the king and the solar cult had been mutually dependent. It was only when the priesthood of Re had become overweeningly powerful and had probably supported a claimant to the throne at a time of dispute in the royal family, that the king had lost his supremacy and had become merely the son of Re.

Any king of Egypt had only to look at the Gizeh pyramids to find inspiration to revive royal divinity; there was no need to look beyond his own country. Neither did he have to create a new god, when the old patron of royalty was still a powerful force. Times had changed however, and such a god would need to acquire elements of internationalism which Amen-Re already expressed, if he were to be made supreme. He would also have to be closely associated with the king and not with his own priesthood, or one set of problems would simply replace another. However, in the minds of the Egyptians and of the king himself, it was the solar cult which was forever linked with the absolute power of the king.

It has been argued that if the Aten cult of the Eighteenth dynasty was indeed a revised form of the old solar worship then why did Akhenaten not simply promote the existing cult of Re? However, there were various sound reasons why an existing and well-established cult could not be used to promote the king's own supremacy and divinity. First, the cult of Re had its own priesthood which had played a considerable part in the diminution of the king's status in the Old Kingdom. To replace the cult of Amun with that of Re as the major state religion would have simply resulted in the ascendancy of a different priesthood. As a major world power, a new supreme deity in Egypt would have to be established as creator and sustainer of peoples who lived beyond the Nile Valley. In the Great Hymn to Amun of Karnak, the international influence of the god is stressed and any god who attempted to replace Amun would have to be similarly far-reaching. The Aten, symbolizing the power which was expressed through the sun but which was not limited to any cult statue or physical form, could readily adopt the role of universal creator of all races.

No one account has been discovered of the philosophy of this cult, but the main concepts have been derived from sources such as the scenes and inscriptions in the private tombs at El-Amarna and the excavated material from Akhetaten itself. In the early stages, the Aten may have been regarded primarily as a special aspect of Re, the old sun god, but the full name of the Aten was soon changed. Mention of Re-Harakhte was removed from the Aten's prenomen and was replaced with the title 'Ruler of the Horizon'; and the word *shu*, which had actually meant 'sunlight' in the context of the Aten's name, was also discarded because it sounded the same as the name of another deity – the god Shu.

The Aten was apparently regarded as a symbol of the creative force of the sun which gave life to all men, animals and plants on earth. This force was beneficient and universal, creating life in regions far beyond the boundaries of Egypt. The famous Hymn to the Aten found in various tombs at El-Amarna shows the far-reaching omnipotence of the god –

Thou art beautiful, great, shining and high above every land, and thy rays enfold the lands to the limit of all that thou hast made, thou being the sun and thou reachest their limits and subjectest them to thy beloved son.

Thou settest every man in his place and makest their sustenance, each one possessing his food, and his term of life counted; tongues made diverse in speech and their characters likewise; their complexions distinguished, for thou hast distinguished country and country.

The uniqueness of the god is also brought out in the hymn –

Thou sole god, like to whom there is none other.

The resemblance between this Hymn and Psalm CIV in the Bible has been noted and much discussed, but although the Hymn to the Aten is couched in fresh and striking terms, it contains little which is really new and which is not contained in earlier Egyptian sun hymns of the New Kingdom. The uniqueness of the Aten finds echoes in earlier poetry to Amen-Re, where the deity is referred to as the 'Sole One'.

However, certain features in the Aten cult are outstanding and some are without precedent either in the earlier years of the New Kingdom, or in Egypt's long history. The Aten and the king appear to have been regarded as almost interchangeable in terms of concept and titles. Akhenaten becomes the sole representative of the god on earth, for there is no priesthood to stand between the king and his god. This is brought out in the many scenes where the Aten is shown as a disc from which rays descend, each ending in a hand, to bestow bounty on the king and his family in return for devotion to the cult. The king is once again a god, as he had been in the days of the Old Kingdom. It was therefore logical that, as when each man, woman and child could look forward to eternity only through the beneficence of their god-king, their hope of everlasting life now rested with Akhenaten. No other god would reign supreme in the underworld as Osiris had done for many centuries. The tomb scenes at El-Amarna replace the gods of the dead and of the underworld with images of the king himself; every effort was apparently made to discard the traditional funerary beliefs and customs at least in these scenes. Some customs were retained but altered – scores of mummiform statuettes, carved in the likeness of the king, were provided and were probably intended to act as *ushabti* figures; they were found near the Royal Tomb at El-Amarna. Also, large scarabs were still inserted inside the mummy wrappings but they were no longer inscribed with the spell from the *Book of the Dead*. This begged the heart to refrain from bearing witness against the deceased when he faced the judgment of his earthly deeds and was a belief closely associated with the Osirian cult. The priests had always gained the dependence of both king and commoners because they controlled and directed the rituals performed at the mortuary temple or in the tomb. Akhenaten would have been fully aware of this, and by making the eternity of his subjects dependent upon the king and not on the funerary gods and their followers, he removed yet another reason for the continued existence of a priesthood.

Perhaps his most dramatic gesture was to demolish the cults and priesthoods of probably all the other deities. Their temples were closed, their names were erased, their priesthoods disbanded, and their revenues diverted to the cult of the Aten. It has been suggested that Atenism was the natural and logical development of an increasing tendency towards monotheism which was particularly evident even in the cult of Amen-Re. However, no previous cult, however powerful, had ever attempted to exclude other Egyptian gods. Other attempts were made to elevate one god, as with Re in the Old Kingdom and with Amen-Re in the New Kingdom, and it has been claimed that Akhenaten's moves were therefore not revolutionary but merely evolutionary – that he simply happened to be the king when events reached this stage and that, whoever had been the ruler at the time, the religious development of the period would have followed the same course. However, the Egyptians themselves reacted strongly against his innovations – the apparent ease and speed with which his successors introduced their counter-revolutionary measures and the hatred with which Akhenaten was regarded by later generations argue against this idea.

What, then, was the character of this man? He has been described as a pacifist who pursued a dream and in so doing, allowed his empire in Asia Minor to slip away. The facts, however, do not entirely confirm this opinion. In the reign of Tuthmosis IV, the Aten is represented as a god of battle, and even in Akhenaten's own reign, some of the contemporary scenes show soldiers were prominent amongst the onlookers at the Royal

Court, and that the King himself appears in some reliefs as a warrior. The extent of the loss of Egypt's empire during this reign has been disputed. Both Akhenaten and his father must have been acutely aware that the 'empire' in Asia Minor was a loose association of vassal states whose allegiance to Egypt could never be fully relied upon, and that no full-scale military expedition to the area would have had any long term effect. Their interest in the region was best served by fostering internal conflict to retain the delicate balance of power, by matrimonial alliances between the Egyptian king and foreign princesses, and by large subsidies of gold. Both rulers outwardly appear to have followed a 'pacifist' policy because they probably realised that military force was not an effective method, but in any case, father and son were both responsible for this policy and its results. Akhenaten also would have wished to consolidate his position and his new cult at home before engaging in conflicts abroad. Even in the Hymn to the Aten, where the god is portrayed as creator of all peoples, there is no doubt that he is seen as the supreme god of Egypt to whom all other countries are subordinate.

Akhenaten's motives in introducing his religious reforms have either been regarded as primarily 'political' and as an attempt to curtail the power of the priests of Amen-Re, or as 'religious', the ill-timed dreams of a fanatic. However, in ancient Egypt, a clear-cut division and interpretation of such terms did not exist; it could be argued that his motives were at the same time both religious and political, and that, through the Aten, he was hoping to establish the absolute power of Egypt's oldest religious and political institution – the monarchy.

More than any other king since those who had enjoyed supreme power in the Fourth dynasty, Akhenaten regarded himself as the ultimate earthly expression of the divinity of the kingship. This concept of kingship was one of the main cornerstones of Egyptian religion, which had survived inter-family strife, political upheavals, foreign occupation and even the rise and fall of many great gods. Not since the pyramid-builders of the Old Kingdom had a king seized such power to make himself not the son of the god but the very earthly embodiment of that deity. Divine kingship was the symbol of religious and political supremacy in Egypt, and it was to this concept that Akhenaten was totally loyal. All his actions are understandable if we concede that this was his dream – to see the king once again as the god of Egypt. Any barriers to his grand concept – such as the existing priesthoods – had to be disbanded and their wealth used to assist the cause.

The pharaohs of the Old Kingdom had built pyramids with associated complexes to provide themselves with the means to achieve eternity, but these had required expensive mortuary cults, dependent on a priesthood. Akhenaten would not have wished to revive this system and no evidence has come to light to suggest that he built a mortuary temple. Indeed, even his father's mortuary temple at Thebes is so completely destroyed that we cannot describe the form it took. Akhenaten did however build himself a different kind of eternal monument in the new city of Akhetaten where, in its temples dedicated to the Aten, he believed his successors would continue to worship the god and thus perpetuate his own memory. He does not state the reason for his departure from Thebes to found his new city other than to imply that it was at the prompting of the god. He may have fled from the hatred of the priests of Amen-Re, or to provide his deity with his own cult centre. There is no suggestion that he quarrelled with his father or mother and indeed they may even have supported his move. If he intended the city to be his own monument, his place of eternity where his descendants would continue the cult of the Aten and thus of himself, it would help to explain why the city was so completely and furiously desecrated after his death.

Akhenaten was certainly regarded as a heretic by later generations. His name was obliterated from the monuments, his reign and that of his immediate successors were discounted in the king lists, his city at El-Amarna was destroyed and his temples at Thebes were demolished. He was remembered with bitterness and hostility and although this may have been encouraged by the reinstated priesthoods of Amen-Re and of the other gods, it may also have been a reaction against a fanatical, even tyrannical man, whose actions upset the established order for the purpose of promoting his own divinity and the power of his family. Although Cheops and Chephren never attempted to introduce anything as extreme as an exclusive cult of the royal god, Re, nevertheless, according to Herodotus, the Greek historian writing in the fifth century BC, later generations regarded them as tyrants. Egyptians of later periods, if not modern historians, seem to have judged Akhenaten even more harshly.

His cult would have had a limited appeal even during Akhenaten's lifetime. Like the old solar cult, it probably only ever had a following at Court, and there was not even a powerful priesthood to support the cult. Aten would have had little attraction for the masses, for, like Re, the god had no physical form in his own sanctuary. As spiritual lord of the universe, the Aten was worshipped as the disc of the sun in the open sky. The god recreated the universe at the start of each day and sustained it with the sun's rays; his creative role was a central theme of the cult reflecting that attributed to the sun god in the Old Kingdom sun temples.

Surely there is no need to look outside Egypt to find the inspiration for this 'new' cult? Akhenaten probably first envisaged the cult as a development closely associated with the old solar worship; this is indicated in his early inscription in the sandstone quarry at Gebel el-Silsileh, where he describes himself as the 'First prophet of Re-Harakhte, Rejoicing-in-his-Horizon, in his name of sunlight which is in Aten'. Finally, however, the god's name is changed, and the Aten is only ever shown in the form of a disc. Soon, Akhenaten and the Aten became interchangeable; they were praised with the same names and phrases. Aten was the king in heaven and Akhenaten was the divine representative on earth; the god and the king were revealed and made manifest in each other, and the success or failure of one would bring about the glory or downfall of the other. Akhenaten also took the title 'Living in Truth', but the exact meaning of this phrase is unclear. It has been interpreted as a desire on his part to be shown in the art of the period as realistically as possible, with his deformities faithfully reproduced and his family gathered around him in informal scenes. Others argue that it underlines his role as the upholder of the cosmic order – the well-regulated system which prevailed throughout the universe, and that anything which opposed the Aten was not 'in truth'. A central element in this principle of 'Ma'at' was the role of the divine pharaoh, who was subject to 'Ma'at', or the laws of the universe, but who held the balance between gods and mankind. By taking such a title, Akhenaten may again have been declaring the essential position of the king.

It has been suggested that the lack of moral philosophy and of a theory of a life after death were serious defects in Atenism which may indicate that Akhenaten could not accept the fact that he would eventually die. However, he did prepare a tomb for himself and his family, and it is more likely that these apparent omissions from the cult can be explained again in terms of the old solar theology. Although each individual ruler would die, the divine kingship would continue for ever. In the early Old Kingdom, the solar theologians claimed that only the king's eternity was clearly defined and that others obtained a vicarious afterlife only through his divine bounty. Only in the Middle Kingdom, when the king had been revealed as less than omnipotent did the funerary beliefs undergo a process of democratization and each individual come to expect a personal chance of eternity. Ethical teaching in Egypt was closely associated with the cult of Osiris and the idea of a 'Day of Judgment', but before this period, the solar cult of the Old Kingdom had contained little practical moral guidance for the ordinary man. The Wisdom Literature had provided some teaching on morals and manners, but this was not part of the cult of the god nor of his mythology or theology. One reason why Atenism failed may have been because Akhenaten discontinued the traditional Osirian ideas of the afterlife and neglected to replace them with another concept. Again, the content of the scenes in the private tombs at El-Amarna could be interpreted as a return to the ideas of the Old Kingdom, with eternity only being achieved through the king's bounty and in his everlasting presence. Whereas once the nobles' tombs had clustered at the base of their lord's pyramid, now they would rest in tombs decorated with scenes showing their king.

The Aten cult seems to have been adopted only by those who wished to advance at Court. These were apparently mostly 'new' men who had followed the young king from Thebes but who had held no positions of honour in the old capital. It is known that the cult had temples elsewhere, but it cannot have become popular, and even at the new capital El-Amarna, in the workmen's village, amulets of traditional symbols and deities, such as the much-loved dwarf god Bes, have been found and indicate that the old beliefs continued. With no cult-statue to be paraded at festivals and no mythology to inspire ordinary people, the Aten failed to make any impact on the masses. We might wonder why Akhenaten did not elect to promote a deity whose form and mythology would have won this support, but surely no god could have had greater appeal than Osiris, with his promise of eternity for all, and Akhenaten's aim to re-establish the divinity of the kingship could only have been achieved through theology and not by consent of the people. There is no evidence to suggest that his memory was effaced as the result of a popular uprising, although the people would have been affected by the religious upheaval, for the closure of the temples

would have deprived many people of menial work and the building of a new city at El-Amarna would have placed a considerable
economic burden on all classes.

Akhenaten's revolution should perhaps be regarded as an
attempt – probably the culmination of a subtle conflict between
king and priests which had existed throughout one or two previous reigns – to re-instate the divinity of the king as accepted in
the Old Kingdom. This concept was tailored to meet new conditions, such as Egypt's relationship with neighbouring countries,
but essentially Akhenaten appears to have attempted to resurrect
the solar cult of the Old Kingdom, removing undesirable elements
such as a powerful priesthood and adding to it the characteristics,
such as universality, which were present in the cult of the great
rival deity, Amun. In these terms, his revolution need not be
considered as exclusively 'religious' or 'political'. It is unlikely that
he was either bent on sweeping his subjects along with him in his
newly found monotheism, or indeed that he and his father carefully and consciously planned and executed the downfall of the
Amun priesthood by developing a powerful new cult. Undoubtedly, the threat of the Amun priests was a major factor in the
events of these two reigns, but Akhenaten's determination to take
his reforms to extremes which no previous king had envisaged
must have been fuelled by an obsessive and fanatical streak in his
character. We cannot determine the influences which moulded his
beliefs although his mother Tiye was undoubtedly a forceful
personality, but she cannot have been openly associated with her
son's most extreme reforms, for both she and her husband were
accorded due reverence by later generations. There can surely be
little doubt that, in the later form of the Aten's name, – 'Re lives,
Ruler of the Horizon, in his name Re the Father who has returned
as Aten' – we have a clear indication that this cult was a revival of
the old solar worship of the Old Kingdom.

The successors of Akhenaten, doubtless guided by those who
had been present at Court throughout this religious upheaval,
were quick to reverse his policies after his death. They may have
realised that the reforms would not be acceptable to Egypt, or
possibly even during Akhenaten's, lifetime they may have disagreed with his tyrannical decisions and bided their time. The city of
Akhetaten was inhabited for less than twenty years and was
incomplete when his successors abandoned it and returned to
Thebes. Later, its final destruction was carried out on the orders of

Horemheb, the one-time courtier of Akhenaten, the buildings were demolished and the stone removed for use elsewhere. Every effort was made to erase his name from inscriptions, the tombs at El-Amarna were desecrated, and the Aten cult was destroyed. The Great Temple was razed to the ground, and statues and reliefs were smashed and piled into heaps outside the southern enclosure wall of the temple. Akhetaten was taken over by the desert sands and by the jackals, and it was only brought to light thousands of years later by the chance discovery of the site and its eventual excavation. Far away to the south, Akhenaten's Theban temples met a similar fate, and knowledge of these buildings was lost until recent times.

However, the re-discovery of this period of Egypt's history has revealed not only a significant era in Egyptian religion but also in the history and development of the art. The name 'El-Amarna' conjures up for many people the distinctive art forms which flourished under the patronage of Akhenaten and which show the only obvious break with tradition throughout the country's long history. Most of the examples come from the city of Akhetaten, where the new king insisted that, in line with his religious beliefs, a more naturalistic art should be attempted. This led to apparently candid portrayals of the king's own physical deformities, which soon become the accepted form for other portraits. Here, again, Akhenaten was perhaps openly flouting the tradition that the king had to be shown to be perfect. Instead he preferred to establish his own abnormalities as the standard which others then had to emulate. If it was his concept of his own divinity as king which motivated his religious reforms, then the apparent peculiarity of the art can be explained in the same way.

In the early years at El-Amarna, the older, more conventional artists were still occupied at Thebes, so Akhenaten had to employ new men at Akhetaten. Even in the reign of Amenophis III, there is some indication of the naturalism which was to follow, as in the statue of Amenophis III showing him as a fat, old man. The tomb of the vizier Ramose at Thebes is one of the most beautiful and interesting of all the Theban private tombs, for although unfinished, the walls of the tomb are decorated with scenes executed in both the traditional and the new Theban styles but at Akhetaten, the king was free to encourage a new generation of craftsmen to develop naturalism almost to a point of caricature, although it is perhaps at its best in the scenes showing the king in the company of his wife and children, and in the paintings of animals, birds and plants. The traditional art had been adopted for use in the tombs, to further the concept of the afterlife, and when this ideology underwent a change, the artists were encouraged instead to create an art form centred on the person of the king.

It seems that Akhenaten was denied the one element which might have ensured the continuation of his life's work – he had no son to embrace his ideals wholeheartedly and succeed him as the divine king. Indeed, even the co-regent, who was probably his younger half-brother, lived for only a short time after Akhenaten's death, and was succeeded by the boy Tutankhaten. His immaturity and inability to continue Akhenaten's policies, even if he had wished to do so, enabled his advisers to steer the country back to traditional paths. Behind the youthful king, the vizier Ay, the army general, Horemheb, and the traditionalists at Court and elsewhere, drew together the threads of conservatism and acted in concert to re-instate the old order.

The Court returned to Thebes, Tutankhaten changed his name to 'Tutankhamun', declaring his allegiance to the old god Amun, and his wife, Ankhesenpaaten, Akhenaten's daughter, took the name of Ankhesenamun. The return to the traditional gods was underlined by Tutankhamun's pious restoration of their old temples and the reconstruction of new sacred buildings. On a large stela near to the third pylon of the Temple of Karnak, he is shown making offerings to Amun and Mut, and he commissioned the decoration of a hall in the Temple of Luxor where wall reliefs show the great Festival of Amen-Re. The temples and priesthoods which Akhenaten had closed and disbanded were now revived.

Nevertheless despite his services to the many gods, the young king met an untimely death at the age of eighteen or nineteen, and his body was buried in a tomb in the Valley of the Kings which had been prepared for another member of the royal family. The discovery and investigation of the tomb and its contents in the early part of this century caused worldwide excitement. The treasures can still be seen in the Cairo Museum where visitors to his tomb can see one of the golden body coffins inside the great sarcophagus, where the body of the young king still rests.

The death of Tutankhamun once again highlighted the problem of the succession, for the king seems to have left no living heir. His widow, the daughter of Akhenaten who had already played an important role in bringing him to the throne, is mentioned once again before disappearing completely from history. She writes to the King of the Hittites, whose strength rivalled Egypt's own position, and asks Suppiluliumas to send his son Zannanza to become her husband. As the royal heiress of Egypt, she would thus confer on this foreign prince the right to rule Egypt. After much delay, the king sends his son, but he is murdered en route, probably by those who did not wish the alliance to take place. Ankhesenamun then marries the elderly courtier Ay, who was possibly her own maternal grandfather, and passes to him the right to rule Egypt. His reign probably lasted for about four years, and he continued the policy of restoration. The tomb he had originally prepared for himself at El-Amarna remained unused, and he elected to be buried at Thebes, where his tomb inscriptions mention only his first wife Tey. We cannot tell what pressures and intrigues prompted Ankhesenamun to take the unprecedented step of offering herself, as queen of Egypt, to become the wife of a foreign prince, but her bold attempt to prevent an Egyptian courtier becoming king was doomed to failure.

The death of Ay again left Egypt without a direct heir, and his successor, the last king of the Eighteenth dynasty, was Horemheb. He was a man of humble origin, whose only claim to the throne was a close association with the royal family throughout many years. It is also possible that his wife, named Mutnodjme, may have been the sister of Nefertiti. He had risen to power from his position as an army commander under the Atenist kings and must have at least paid lip service to Akhenaten's reforms. Perhaps, at first, he genuinely supported the king's innovations before they became extreme, but he eventually became dedicated to the destruction of all that pertained to the Aten heresy. He was responsible for the dismantling of Akhetaten and Akhenaten's temples at Thebes, incorporating the blocks as infill material in the traditional temples there.

His years as vice-regent had given him the opportunity to gain experience and as king, his sympathies rested with the soldiers and the priests. He re-introduced a strong, aggressive army and a new and powerful priesthood who relied on him for appointment. A stela by the side of the tenth pylon in the Temple of Karnak is inscribed with a copy of his restoration decree. Although badly damaged, this indicates that his rehabilitation of temples and their priests and properties was widespread. He ruled for at least twenty-seven years, and was regarded by later generations as the next legitimate king after Amenophis III, whose name he follows in the King Lists. Intervening rulers were apparently all associated in the minds of the Egyptians with the Aten heresy.

Horemheb had prepared a tomb at Saqqara, probably before there was any likelihood that he would become king, but his kingly tomb was made ready at Thebes. He left behind a country where, at least superficially, the old order had been restored; he had reorganized the army and the law-courts, and the priesthood had been re-instated, although the men were not picked from the old families, but were frequently drawn from the army. The throne now passed to his comrade, his old commander-at-arms, Pa-Ramesses. This man was the son of a troop-commander named Sethy. Pa-Ramesses became King Ramesses I, the inaugurator of the Nineteenth dynasty, and although his reign was brief, his son and descendants brought to Egypt a new era of power and prosperity. They made every effort to expunge the memory of the hated heretic and to assert their loyalty and gratitude to Egypt's many gods.

Akhenaten had tried to transform the king into a supreme and exclusive god, so that he would be raised on a pinnacle above the clamouring demands and rivalry of the priests. With no roots either in a popular following or in its own powerful priesthood, the survival of the cult was dependent on the momentum created by Akhenaten and ultimately on a continuing line of omnipotent god-kings. Akhenaten died before the continuation of the cult could be ensured, and his immediate successors were minor rulers who left no heirs.

It is tempting to regard this interlude, with its overtones of monotheism and pacifism, as a tragic failure, and to see the counter-revolutionaries as men who curtailed an experiment which might have brought religious 'enlightenment' to the polytheistic Egyptians. However, it is probably more valid to regard this as an attempt by one man to secure forever, for himself and his descendants, the absolute and divine status of the king; to this end, he was prepared to devote all his actions, even at the expense of destroying the fundamental beliefs of many people. The Egyptians of later generations, who, unlike us, saw Akhenaten in the context of their own times and religious beliefs, made every effort to efface his name and to destroy his memory; they certainly did not regard him as a 'failed messiah' nor even as a shrewd politician.

# *Epilogue*

The Amarna period was the only time when the solar cult was interpreted as a form of monotheism. After the counter-revolution, there was a return to traditional beliefs and customs and, at least superficially, the cult of the Aten passed into oblivion. The religious centre remained at Thebes, where the priesthood of Amen-Re lost no time in attempting to gain political power, but the political capital and main royal residence was now situated at one of the northern sites which was more centrally placed to foster Egypt's renewed ambitions in Asia Minor.

By the end of the Twentieth dynasty, the priests of Amen-Re once again wielded great strength and influence, and the High Priest of Amen-Re at Karnak, a man named Herihor, was in a sufficiently strong position to found a theocracy at Thebes. He was able to vest in himself all the state roles of the king, and even to hand these on to his descendants. In the precincts of the Temple of Karnak, he assumed the status of ruler, but he could not extend his rule outside Karnak since the pharaoh, Ramesses XI, was still alive. A situation developed whereby Herihor and his priestly descendants ruled from Thebes, the religious capital in the south, while the true kings ruled from the northern capital of Tanis. There was apparently no breakdown in relationships between the two centres, and indeed, the families were even linked by ties of marriage and friendship.

Amen-Re again became a supremely powerful god, although there was never any attempt to pursue a policy similar to that of Akhenaten where other gods were desecrated. The god's importance was promoted by accentuating his unique nature and role as the creator of all other deities, but less emphasis was placed on his solar characteristics. He became again a powerful god of the empire, and his use in oracles whereby political decisions were reached gave him an additional function.

The Twenty-first dynasty, based on government from two capitals, was replaced by a new situation in which Egypt was ruled by a line of foreign dynasts. These were not invaders, as the Hyksos had been; they were probably the descendants of settlers or captured Libyan prisoners who, in return for undertaking military service on behalf of Pharaoh, had been given land in Egypt. These rulers of the Twenty-second dynasty appear to have taken over from the kings of the Twenty-first dynasty on amicable terms, and they established their capital city at Tanis or Bubastis in the Delta. Throughout this period, the priests of Amen-Re at Thebes retained their status although the next line of rulers to enter Egypt were to extend the influence of this god even further.

During the earlier part of the Eighteenth dynasty, when Amen-Re had been the great state god of Egypt, and the empire had stretched from Nubia in the south to parts of Asia Minor in the north, the Egyptians had established one of several colonies in Nubia. The area had its provincial capital at Napata, and here, throughout the troublesome times that followed, the people retained an isolated community with Egyptian customs and nurtured their faith in Amen-Re. The rulers of this area now decided to enter Egypt from the south, perhaps to restore to full glory the cult of Amen-Re at Thebes, and the period of their kingship over Egypt coincides with the Twenty-fifth dynasty.

These southern kings are often referred to as 'Ethiopians' or 'Napatans', and a feature of their rule was their adopting as a political instrument an aspect of the existing Theban theocracy. This was the title and role of the 'God's Wife'. In previous periods, this title had been given to the king's wife, but in the Twenty-first dynasty, it was transferred to the king's daughter, who became the wife of the god Amun and was forbidden to marry or to bear children. Because his daughter held this most important position at Thebes, the king could make certain that there was no important male rival in the southern capital, and the rulers of the Twenty-fifth dynasty took this a step further by insisting that the daughter of the ruling king should be adopted by the daughter of the previous king, as her successor at Thebes. The God's Wife was all-important at Thebes, where she passed the whole of her life;

she could own great estates and many servants and could even present offerings to the gods, but her great influence was confined to Thebes. The king could rest assured that, with his daughter supreme at Thebes, no rival to his power would take over the southern capital, and her unmarried state would prevent his position being threatened by her husband or children.

Fervent worshippers of Amen-Re, the kings of the Twenty-fifth dynasty encouraged his cult to flourish, but when the Assyrians invaded Egypt from the north and finally subdued Thebes in 663 BC, the Ethiopian rulers fled back to the south. Amen-Re had been identified for so many years with the national cult of Egypt that any foreign invader would make every attempt to lessen the god's hold on the country. The following centuries saw the conquest of Egypt by the armies of the Persians, of Alexander the Great, and eventually by the Romans. The solar cult had always been closely associated with the Egyptian king and these conquerors now neglected the cult in favour of that of Osiris who had always been a personal god rather than a symbol of national pride. Thus, the solar cult, embodied in the worship of Amen-Re, finally faded away.

The last remnants of the worship of this great Egyptian god and the symbols most closely associated with the solar cult lingered on beyond Egypt's southernmost boundaries. The Ethiopian rulers of the Twenty-fifth dynasty whom the Assyrians had driven from Egypt returned to their southern kingdom of Napata. During the Twenty-fifty dynasty, one of these rulers named Piankhy had revived the ancient custom, long since discontinued in Egypt, of building the royal tomb in the shape of a pyramid, and at Kuru, near Napata, he had erected a pyramid as his burial place. When these kings returned to Napata, and all political contact between Egypt and their kingdom ceased, they pursued the custom of being buried in pyramids at Kuru and Napata and building smaller pyramids for their queens and princes. A new capital was eventually established at Meroë, to the south, and these rulers continued to build pyramids, and to foster, in isolation, many of the features of Egyptian civilization. Here, the solar cult, which had flourished for so many centuries in Egypt and which had been so closely interwoven with the concept of divine kingship, finally disappeared forever.

# Glossary

The long history of Egypt is divided into thirty-one dynasties, following the scheme of Manetho, an Egyptian priest, who wrote a history of Egypt (in Greek) around 250 BC. For greater convenience these dynasties are grouped into a small number of periods, shown in the table below, together with the preceding and succeeding non-dynastic periods:

Predynastic period c. 5000–3100BC
Archaic period (Dyn. I and II) 3100–2686BC
Old Kingdom (Dyn. III–VI) 2686–2181BC
First Intermediate period (Dyn. VII–XI) 2181–1991BC
Middle Kingdom (Dyn. XII) 1991–1786BC
Second Intermediate period (Dyn. XIII–XVII) 1786–1552BC
New Kingdom (Dyn. XVIII–XX) 1552–1069BC
Third Intermediate period (Dyn. XXI–XXVI) 1069–525BC
Late period (Dyn. XXVII–XXXI) 525–332BC
Conquest by Alexander the Great 332BC
Period of Greek rule (Ptolemaic period) 332–30BC
Roman period 30BC–AD641
Islamic conquest AD641

The three greatest periods of Egyptian history are, as their names imply, the Old, Middle, and New Kingdoms. The period before Dynasty I is known as the Predynastic period.

# Select Bibliography

Sir Alan Gardiner *Egypt of the Pharaohs* (Oxford 1974)

I. E. S. Edwards *The Pyramids of Egypt* (London 1972)

W. C. Hayes *The Scepter of Egypt*, 2 vols (New York & Cambridge, Mass. 1953–9)

G. E. Smith and W. R. Dawson *Egyptian Mummies* (London 1904)

E. Thomas 'Solar Barks Prow to Prow' in *J.E.A.* 42 (1956), pp. 65–79, 117–18

F. W. von Bissing *Das Re-Heiligtum des Königs Ne-Woser-Re* 3 vols (Berlin and Leipzig 1905–28)

W. B. Emery *Archaic Egypt* (London 1972)

K. Mendelssohn *The Riddle of the Pyramids* (London 1974)

H. Ricke 'Erster Grabungsbericht über das Sonnenheiligtum des Königs Userkaf bei Abusir' in *A.S.A.E.* vol. LIV (1956–7), pp. 75–82

'Zweiter Grabungsbericht über das Sonnenheiligtum des Königs Userkaf bei Abusir' in *A.S.A.E.* vol. LIV (1956–7), pp. 305–16

'Dritter Grabungsbericht über das Sonnenheiligtum des Königs Userkaf bei Abusir' in *A.S.A.E.* vol. LIV (1956–7), pp. 73–7

A. R. David *A Guide to Abydos* (forthcoming title, Warminster 1979/80)

C. Aldred *Akhenaten* (London 1968)

C. Aldred *Akhenaten and Nefertiti* (New York 1973)

N. de G. Davies *The Rock Tombs of El-Amarna* (London 1908)

C. Desroches-Noblecourt *Tutankhamen* (London 1963)

A. H. Gardiner 'The So-Called Tomb of Queen Tiye' in *J.E.A.* 43 (1957), pp. 10–25

C. Aldred 'The Tomb of Akhenaten at Thebes' in *J.E.A.* 47 (1961), pp. 41–65

R. G. Harrison 'An Anatomical Examination of the Pharaonic Remains purported to be Akhenaten' in *J.E.A.* 52 (1966), pp. 95–119

R. Winfield Smith and D. B. Redford *The Akhenaten Temple Project* vol. 1: Initial Discoveries (Warminster 1976)

*Abbreviations*

J.E.A. – Journal of Egyptian Archaeology
A.S.A.E. – Annales du Service des Antiquités de l'Égypte

# Index